Children's Rooms

HOW TO DECORATE THEM TO GROW WITH YOUR CHILD

BY
Ellen Levine

BOBBS-MERRILL

Indianapolis/New York

*ISBN 0-672-51938-0
Library of Congress Catalog Card Number: 74-17662
Designed by Irving Perkins and Helen Barrow
Manufactured in the United States of America*

First printing

To My Family

Thanks to my friends who encouraged me from the inception of the book's outline through to the end of Chapter 11 —especially to Carol Plaine, Marilyn Houston, Sharon Gold, Gloria Levine, Karen Bruno and Sandra Schanzer. And special thanks to my mother, Jean Jacobson, who read every word despite the attempts of her grandchildren to distract her—and whose innate good taste made her a great critic.

CREDITS

Credit is due to the following for pictures used in this book:

Page 14. *Top*, David Laurence Roth. *Bottom*, Collins & Aikman.

Page 15. Jane Victor Associates.

Page 22. *Top left*, Bassett Furniture. *Top right*, Saks Fifth Avenue. *Bottom*, Child Craft.

Page 23. *Top*, Child Craft. *Bottom*, Children's Workbench.

Page 24. *Top*, Waverly Fabrics. *Bottom*, Cosco.

Page 25. Sears, Roebuck and Company.

Page 26. *Top*, Evans Paneling. *Bottom*, Celanese Corporation and the Window Shade Manufacturers Association.

Page 27. Monarch Carpet Mills.

Page 32. *Top left*, Joseph Braswell. *Top right*, Bachstein & Lawrence. *Bottom*, Imperial Wallpaper.

Page 33. Burlington Domestics.

Page 34. Simmons Company.

Page 35. *Top*, Window Shade Manufacturers Association. *Bottom*, Celanese Corporation.

Page 36. *Top*, Regal Rugs. *Bottom*, Simmons Company.

Page 37. Window Shade Manufacturers Association.

Page 38. Window Shade Manufacturers Association.

Page 39. Abraham & Straus.

Page 40. Salvatore Cesararie.

Page 41. *Top*, Window Shade Manufacturers Association. *Bottom*, Dorothy Baker Billings.

Page 42. *Top*, Syroco. *Bottom*, Scotchgard Fabric Protector.

Page 43. *Top*, Ruben de Saavedra. *Bottom*, Imperial Wallpaper.

Page 44. *Top*, Martin Kuckly. *Bottom*, Window Shade Manufacturers Association.

Page 48. *Top*, Gerda Clark/Abraham & Straus. *Bottom*, JS/Permaneer.

Page 49. *Top*, JS/Permaneer. *Bottom*, Jane Victor Associates.

Page 50. *Top*, Window Shade Manufacturers Association. *Bottom*, Evans Paneling.

Page 51. *Top*, Comark Division, United Merchants & Manufacturers. *Bottom*, Evans Paneling.

Page 52. *Top*, Cosco Contemporaries. *Center*, Sherman-Williams Paint. *Bottom*, Simmons Company.

Page 53. Celanese Corporation.

Page 54. Evans Paneling.

Page 55. *Top*, Simmons Company. *Bottom*, Evans Paneling.

Page 56. Imperial Wallpaper.

Page 57. *Top*, Window Shade Manufacturers Association. *Bottom*, Gerda Clark/Abraham & Straus.

Page 58. *Left*, Celanese Corporation. *Right*, Jane Victor Associates.

Page 61. Celanese Corporation.

Page 62. *Top*, Simmons Company. *Bottom*, National Cotton Council.

Page 63. T. Miles Gray.

Page 64. Gerda Clark/Abraham & Straus.

Page 65. Gerda Clark/Abraham & Straus.

Page 66. *Top*, Fieldcrest. *Bottom*, Hercules Incorporated.

Page 71. *Top*, West Point Pepperell. *Bottom*, Window Shade Manufacturers Association.

Page 72. GAF Corporation.

Page 73. Gerda Clark/Abraham & Straus.

Page 74. *Top left*, Window Shade Manufacturers Association. *Top right*, Fieldcrest. *Bottom*, Comark Division, United Merchants & Manufacturers.

Page 75. Wallcovering Industry Bureau.

Page 76. Fieldcrest.

Page 77. *Top*, Celanese Corporation.

Page 78. *Top left*, Window Shade Manufacturers Association. *Top right*, Armstrong. *Bottom*, Fieldcrest.

Pages 82-85. Celanese Corporation.

Page 93. *Top*, Ruben de Saavedra. *Bottom*, Armstrong.

Page 94. Hercules Incorporated.

Page 95. Egetaepper Rugs.

Page 96. *Top*, Window Shade Manufacturers Association.

Page 97. *Left*, Masonite. *Right*, Fieldcrest.

Page 98. Blanche Goodman.

Page 99. Celanese Corporation.

Page 100. *Top*, Sears, Roebuck and Company. *Bottom*, Stanley Furniture.

Page 101. Sears, Roebuck and Company.

Page 105. *Top and bottom*, Living Module Inc. *Center*, Abraham & Straus. *Bottom left*, J. Josephson Wallcoverings.

Page 106. *Top*, Simmons Company. *Bottom*, Mr. Sandman.

Page 107. *Top*, Schoolfield Furniture. *Bottom*, Mr. Sandman.

Page 108. *Top*, Bloomingdale's, New York. *Bottom*, Mr. Sandman.

Page 109. *Top*, Children's Workbench. *Bottom*, Living Modules Inc.

Page 110. Simmons Company.

Page 113. Celanese Corporation.

Page 114. J. Josephson.

Page 115. *Top*, Lees Carpet. *Bottom*, Window Shade Manufacturers Association.

Page 116. *Top left*, Imperial Wallcoverings. *Bottom left*, Waverly Fabrics. *Right*, Joanna Western Mills Co.

Page 117. *Top*, Du Pont. *Bottom*, Armstrong.

Page 118. St. Mary's.

Page 119. *Right*, Celanese Corporation. *Left*, James Seeman Studios.

Page 120. *Top*, Celanese Corporation. *Bottom*, Fieldcrest.

Page 121. Sears, Roebuck and Company.

Page 122. *Right*, Eastman Chemical Products. *Left*, Du Pont Company.

Page 123. *Top*, GAF Corporation. *Bottom*, Celanese Corporation.

TABLE OF CONTENTS

INTRODUCTION

Raising children is a cooperative venture with an investment of love, understanding, and plain old hard work. Decorating a home that reflects your family's life style takes much the same effort. The end result of both should be a mixture of pride, pleasure, and fun. And of all the rooms in your home that should be the most fun and require the least financial commitment, the children's room takes first place.

As soon as a baby is expected the nursery plans begin. When a move to a new home is contemplated the children's room is discussed over and over again. This is true for several reasons. A child's room can be decorated inexpensively, easily, and creatively. But most important, a child must be settled at home to have a sense of security. The idea for this book germinated shortly after my first child was born. I hunted for just the right advice on what I needed to make my baby's special world exciting, stimulating, and comfortable. There was no book available so I had to go it alone.

Decorating books have been written about every other room in the house, but none has been devoted to the children's room, none to those stages of development in a young child's life.

Children react, just as adults do, to their surroundings. A bright yellow room is more likely to make them cheerful and gay. A monotone neutral room will elicit no response. Psychologists tell us that the early years in a person's life are the key to his success in life. In decorating your children's room you are doing more than just creating a handsome setting. You are expressing your feelings and creating an environment that will teach them things about themselves as well as about life. A neat room will teach children what order means. A room with art will introduce them to aesthetics.

Best of all, decorating your child's room takes more ingenuity than money. There are many quick and easy projects and budget ideas with style.

This book is for beginners—even those with no decorating knowledge, living in cramped quarters, coping with a strict budget. All you need is love.

GETTING STARTED

The single most exciting challenge about creating a room for your child is that the child represents a beginning, a fresh start. Children are vital, happy, alive. In planning a room for your child you're bound to succeed as long as you keep one basic thing in mind—the child. The room is meant to cater to your child's needs. The room will grow with the child, changing as his needs dictate, keeping pace with, even promoting, his advances and achievements.

CONSIDER THE ROOM

Who's afraid of a big, bare room? Almost everyone! It's comforting to know that you're not in the minority if you feel overwhelmed by the supposedly simple task of pulling together an attractive room for your youngster. Calm yourself. A basic guideline will aid you in organizing yourself and planning the room.

Basic Guide to Room Decorating

1. Make a floor plan.
2. Consider the function of the room.
3. Plan the layout on a floor plan.
4. Consider the color.
5. Budget your expenses.

The fun of decorating will begin after you have accomplished these elementary exercises. First, you will want to consider the room. To really understand the room and how it will function, you must make a floor plan of the existing space taking into account all the architectural features, such as placement of radiators, wall turns, windows, closets, doors and how they swing open. This will give you a bird's-eye perspective of the outlines of the room.

To make the floor plan your materials will be:

pad of graph paper
ruler
pencil
scissors
lightweight cardboard or construction paper

Depending on the size of your graph paper and the size of the room, you may use either a scale of ½″ to 1′ or ¾″ to 1′. That will translate easily—a room 10′ by 15′ on the ½″ scale will measure 5″ by 7½″ on the graph paper.

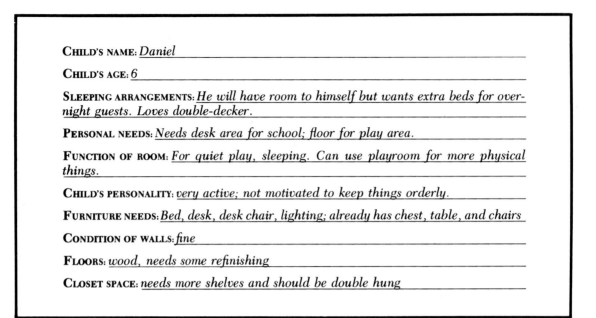

CHILD'S NAME: *Daniel*

CHILD'S AGE: *6*

SLEEPING ARRANGEMENTS: *He will have room to himself but wants extra beds for overnight guests. Loves double-decker.*

PERSONAL NEEDS: *Needs desk area for school; floor for play area.*

FUNCTION OF ROOM: *For quiet play, sleeping. Can use playroom for more physical things.*

CHILD'S PERSONALITY: *very active; not motivated to keep things orderly.*

FURNITURE NEEDS: *Bed, desk, desk chair, lighting; already has chest, table, and chairs*

CONDITION OF WALLS: *fine*

FLOORS: *wood, needs some refinishing*

CLOSET SPACE: *needs more shelves and should be double hung*

Next, measure the length, width, and height of the room, taking note of the placement of all architectural features in these measurements. Be precise. Accuracy really does count. You will transfer these measurements to the graph paper for your floor plan. The floor plan will be your guide to what you will order for the room. You wouldn't want to order carpeting that doesn't cover the floor or wallpaper that doesn't quite make it—just because your initial measurements were off by a foot.

Once you have the skeletal outlines of the room down on paper, it's time to assess the basic function of the room. This, of course, depends on both the child's and the entire family's needs. If you are living in a small apartment, the child's room will be more than just a sleeping area. He will play there, work there, rest there.

If the home is spacious enough to provide a playroom and a backyard, the room will have a different role. Help yourself understand the room's functions with a chart such as the one following. This will be of infinite value to you in determining just what pieces of furniture you must buy, and how to use your existing floor space advantageously.

No matter how many demands you would like to put on a room, there is a limit to what it can take. You will want to find out just what the room can confortably accommodate in furniture. This is when your floor plan comes in handy. Using cardboard or construction paper (again in scale with the floor plan), cut out templates or small facsimiles of the furnishings for the room. In a nursery, for example, these basics would include a crib, chair, changer or dressing table, and perhaps a day bed. The teenager's room would require one or two beds, a desk and chair, bookshelves, chest of drawers. After you arrange these on the floor plan you will literally see whether or not there is room left for extras that the design scheme might call for.

CONSIDER THE COLOR

Now comes the fun. After all that painstaking preparation it's time to choose the colors. Life is your palette. You may pick almost any color combination that pleases you—and your child if he is old enough to be consulted. Anyone from five years up has a right to cast a vote in favor of the color he will live with. This also is the point where you will want to take into account a number of elementary decorating rules that might apply to this decision. Colors have a way of accentuating the negative and eliminating the positive if used without caution.

1. The room will affect your color selection. If it is a bright sunny room with a southern exposure rather than a northern one you need not use color for a pick up. In dark rooms you will want to keep things bright and light to compensate for the lack of natural light.

2. Dark colors will ordinarily make a small room seem smaller. Light colors will make the room seem larger.

3. Light colors tend to make things disappear. Dark, more intense colors attract attention. For example, a dark color will give the illusion of lowering a high ceiling. A light color will make it seem higher.

4. Color can camouflage. If a radiator is an eyesore, for instance, paint it the same color as the background of the room, even if the room is apple green. Beginners often make the mistake of painting objects like the radiator or a pipe the same color as the trim (that is, doors, window frames, moldings). That will accentuate the negative, as mentioned.

5. Colors should relate to each other in the room. If you want to paint one wall cherry red, great! Just make sure you use cherry red again in the room either in accents, on the floor, or in fabric selections.

HOW TO CHOOSE THE COLOR

It's time to make your first decision. You know what intensities of color your room needs. Let's plan a color scheme. Pick your colors from any inspiration.

To get an idea of the possibilities, consider these selections:

1. Designer Jane Victor was working on a scheme for a child's room and came up with a particularly sweet idea. She colored the room with the delicious tones of lollypop flavors.

2. A floral centerpiece with an array of spring fresh flowers—anemones, daisies, and tulips—was the starting point for a teenage haven.

3. The seasons are obvious color palettes. Winter white contrasts with evergreen and gray. The autumn tones can have equally sophisticated arrays of hues. Summer brings to mind sand, ocean, sky, and vivid leaf green.

4. A wallpaper or fabric pattern may give you just the colors you want. Even a sheet may be the color key. Designer Bebe Winkler picked up the tones from a muted pastel patchwork sheet for a teenager's room.

5. A beautiful painting or a poster may be your personal inspiration.

USING THE COLOR

For the sake of discussion, let's say you picked three colors to work with—red, white, and blue, which also happens to be the most popular color scheme for children's rooms. It will help you to plan a balanced design if you visualize the room as having six surfaces—the four walls, the ceiling, and the floor.

You might opt to balance the six surfaces by dividing them into two and two and two. For example, the ceiling and one wall might be painted white, two other walls painted a gloss

PICTURE DESCRIPTIONS OVERLEAF

Refreshing sherbert flavors brighten these young girls' rooms.
In the raspberry pink room, *top*, designer David
Laurence Roth combines four patterns keeping pink the
primary color.
Lime sherbert unifies the room that sisters share, *bottom*.
The delicious green color is laced with white and punctuated with
strawberry red for a look that promises summer year round.

Vibrant red, white, and blue colors this stimulating room for twin
boys. Designer Jane Victor takes this common color scheme (the
most popular for children's rooms) and treats it with originality
mixing patterns and accenting the unexpected such as a red ceiling
dotted with white lights.

red, and the remaining wall and floor covered in a blue.

Take that basic theme and try an original variation—orange, blue, and white. Just by substituting the orange in place of the red you will give the room an offbeat effect.

A combination of pink and orange might be your choice. A shag rug in orange and pink for the floor can be color matched with a whimsical orange and pink and white wallpaper. The trim should be painted a gloss orange or pink—whichever you prefer to emphasize. The ceiling remains a conventional white.

One of the most important points in coordinating your child's room is to plan ahead. That means think before you buy. You will want to make sure you can find an orange and pink print to match that shag rug before you order the rug. If the rug goes down first and the orange just doesn't match anything, the entire room becomes a problem. Take a tip from the professionals here. They always ask for small color swatches of carpet selections, wallpaper, and paint to make sure it's a match and not a clash. Carry these samples with you stapled or pinned to a small memo pad along with descriptions of room dimensions, yardages required, names and addresses of sources.

You might also try living with these samples. If you can get a large enough cutting of fabric or wallpaper, hang it up in the room for a while to make sure you really like it.

WHAT NOW?

You know what the room is like—you have a clear picture in your mind and on paper of the layout. You know what you need in furniture to make it function. You know what colors you want and like. It's time to take an account of accounting. A youngster's room should not have to cost any more than you can afford. What you will spend depends, of course, on your budget, but there are other practical considerations involved in planning the room that will save you time and trouble and cost you less in the long run.

One of the most important pieces of advice, and this holds true in all aspects of decorating, is the timeworn adage that you get what you pay for. With the exception of legitimate sales and second-hand bargains, a "steal" may end up costing you more. If you decide that you want to buy a dresser for the nursery and you want this piece of furniture to grow with the child, lasting well through his teen years, buy quality. A well-constructed chest made of durable materials will better withstand the wear and tear inflicted by a growing child.

Try to resist the temptation to invest in frills and gimmicks. There's probably nothing more enchanting than designing a youngster's room around a double-decker bed modeled after an English bus. Adorable, yes. Enduring, no! As cute as it is at the moment, your child will outgrow it about the time he heads into his teens, if not sooner. If your budget is limited, this is just not the kind of extravagance you can afford. If you are a handy home carpenter, though, you might manage to create your own home grown variety. See Chapter 11 for some easy projects.

Remember the life of the room. If you are in a house and plan to stay there for many years it makes excellent sense to carpet or wallpaper. If a moving date is in mind put your money where it really counts—in furnishings that you will be able to take with you.

Always buy from reputable dealers. Fly-by-night operations will not be there when you have complaints. Established dealers will stand by what they sell.

CHAPTER

IN THE NURSERY

The nursery has come a long way since the days when design was dictated by the Mother Goose School of Decorating. Power blue and pastel pink, those perennial nursery color schemes, have given way to vibrant and unorthodox combinations of primary reds, blues, and yellows.

What's more, the break-away spirit influencing today's nursery is grounded in fact. While an infant is spending his youngest days in his crib he is investigating, as best he can, the small world around him—the walls, the ceiling, the crib. Psychologists have found that children are stimulated and their curiosity developed quite soon after they are born. They literally thrive on what they can see, hear, and feel. Their own room will give them a message of warmth and love.

In decorating your youngster's first world there's much to keep in mind. You should try to make it as exciting as you can, as safe as possible, and as pleasant and cheerful as your imagination permits—leaving plenty of room for the room to grow with your child.

HOW TO PLAN A ROOM THAT WILL GROW

Infancy is only twelve short months and you certainly don't want the nursery outdated that soon. Thinking and planning ahead will allow the room to grow with your child.

There is no reason why your child should outgrow anything in his room besides the crib. The room should be sophisticated enough to stand on its own after the crib is replaced by a bed and after his interests evolve from nursery rhymes to reality. There are more "don'ts" to consider then "dos."

1. Don't waste money by investing in juvenile furniture. If you buy solid, well-designed storage units they will become a mainstay in your youngster's room.

2. Don't install wallpaper or vinyl or linoleum flooring with nursery motifs—unless you don't mind spending time and money again on the background in a couple of years.

3. Don't spend too much on the crib if the budget is limited.

4. Don't use pastels as the color scheme—unless they are your only alternatives. Infants will outgrow pale tones as fast as they grow out of their layettes.

5. Put your money where it will continue to work for you and your child—in good furniture, a second twin-size bed, long-lasting window and floor treatments.

NURSERY NEEDS

Like any other room in the house the nursery demands certain essentials—a combination of the infant's needs and the mother's requirements. First on the list is the crib—the one object that defines the room as a nursery. Other baby equipment requirements include a changing table, a chair, a chest of drawers, perhaps an extra bed.

The Crib

Until a few years ago choosing a crib was a relatively easy matter. You might vacillate between a wood or painted finish and plain or fancy crib rails. But that was that. Now there are so many innovative styles available, the crib has become a major decorative purchase.

The old favorite, the upright crib on legs with sides that go up and down and a mattress that can be lowered, is still the number one choice. This comes in many different finishes, painted, wood, antiqued, and embellished with a design motif or fabric trim. The new look of today comes through in lucite cribs (very expensive), brass cribs (decorator's dreams and also expensive), creative child styles (crib-in-the-round) and Scandinavian modern cribs (low slung in blond woods).

The painted crib has a decided advantage in longevity. It can always be repainted to look like new. The Scandinavian cribs are generally smaller (though not less costly) than the American cribs and are worth considering if you are cramped for space. Because they are close to the floor you will find yourself bending over a great deal while the baby is young, but once he is old enough to stand, the "on-the-floor" crib has a safety plus—if baby throws himself out of the crib or falls trying to climb out he won't fall far. A few of these models convert to benches when crib days are over.

The decorator cribs such as the brass imports are pretty to look at and real attention getters. The price will also get a lot of attention! But if money isn't the question, make sure you ask certain questions.

If you plan to have several children, you'll want a crib sturdy enough to last at least ten years. Will this crib make it? Does the crib collapse? If it doesn't, storing it will be a big headache. Are the slats far apart? If the slats or rails are too far apart the baby may hurt himself by wedging his head between the rails. Babies do a lot of unexpected things. Does the side go up and down? If not, you'll get a lot of unnecessary exercise lifting your child out of bed. And six pound babies grow up to thirty pounds before they get out of the crib.

If someone in your family offers to give or to lend you a crib you might want to say yes. If it is in good working order you can make it like new by buying a new mattress, not a major purchase, and refinishing the crib to freshen it up and coordinate it with your scheme. *Caution: Make sure in refinishing or painting the crib that the paint or varnish you use is guaranteed to be safe for children with no lead content that may harm the infant.* A crib becomes a giant teething ring for about one year of a child's life and he will be very adept at gumming off large areas of paint.

Another crib to consider if you are space hungry or married to two homes is the Port-A-Crib, an easy-to-fold crib with a thin mattress. This is good for a short term but not strong enough to take several years of constant use.

Crib costs: A crib from a well-known manufacturer will start at about $50. Custom-made decorator models go as high as $200 and up.

The Changing or Dressing Table

The other basic nursery "must" is a place to dress and diaper the infant. The changing table comes in a variety of models from the foldable wicker versions to the more substantial wood models. If you can afford a changer it will make nursery days more convenient (the changer also provides a place to store diapers and other baby sundries). If budget or space limitations make a changer out of the question you may accomplish the same purpose by placing a thin carriage size mattress on top of a chest of drawers. And for your own personal comfort, modify the height of the changer if it does not accommodate you. If you are short you may want to cut down the legs. Adding a foam slab will build up the height for taller than average mothers.

Furniture and Fabrics

For the first months of infancy the furniture in the nursery will be geared toward the mother's needs. A chair is essential. The ideal chair for these early months is a rocker. It is a marvelous place to feed the infant and comfort him during those fretful hours.

But once baby crawls a rocker can be a hazard. He may catch his fingers under the rockers or tip the entire chair over on himself. Whatever chair you select you will also want a small companion table next to it. This will be the place you will rest the bottle and warmer while burping.

Another nursery item is a twin bed. It's a great convenience for a worried parent when baby is sick. Make sure the bedspread is washable or easy to dry clean.

You will not need a chest of drawers the min-

ute your baby comes home from the hospital. But by the time he's out of layette wear you will find yourself short of storage space. A simple chest of drawers in a painted, unpainted, or wood finish is what you want. The nursery chests, commodes, and armoires decorated with decals and wood relief figures will not take your child through his teens. If you can get the chest with a Formica surface, so much the better. To adapt the chest to your nursery plans, if you feel you must, simply change the drawer pulls to a nursery theme and replace them later.

Furniture for your child caters to his needs. As an infant he will need only the crib. But when he is two years old he will be ready for a place to sit and crayon or read. The answer: a child-size table and chairs. As with all nursery furniture the table and chairs should be sturdy. You may wish to buy a set. These are available in bright molded plastics or more traditional wood models with whimsical shapes and designs. A handy parent can make the table by cutting down the legs of an old end table or building up the height of a cocktail table to accommodate your child's size.

Lighting

Overhead lighting, ideally on a reostat or dimmer, provides adequate illumination for a nursery. From a safety point of view it eliminates lamps therefore eliminating the problems of cords for baby to chew on or trip over. You may want to place a pole lamp near the changer for better and more direct light. And, of course, there's always the night light—as much the parent's need as the child's.

DECORATING THE ROOM

When you outline your nursery designs, remember the room is for the child. It is meant to be safe, secure, cheerful, and childproof. The toddler should not have to be reprimanded everytime he spills something, jumps on the bed, or tosses his pillows on the floor. The room is not meant to be a showcase of romantic fantasies with yards of organdy frills and expensive fragile fabrics. Fragile fabrics may be pretty but they're wrong for the child. With today's materials you needn't impose a "hands off" policy. It's possible to find fabrics and furniture that can be easily washed and cleaned.

Aside from very elementary layout considerations (you won't want the crib too close to a radiator or window) designing the nursery is an exercise in imagination. And you may begin arranging your floor plan as explained in Chapter 1.

Color

Color is the single most important ingredient in the room. Consider what will interest your baby and what pleases you but don't worry about the baby's sex in a color choice. Navy blue is no more a boy's color than yellow is a girl's. Remember: strong colors are more exciting and inviting to children. The wispy pastels can't keep up with the competition.

Where does color belong? Color belongs anywhere and everywhere. The walls are a logical focal point. Wallpaper is an excellent investment for a nursery, providing your landlord agrees. It is an obvious and entertaining way of introducing color and pattern at the same time. A washable vinyl paper will last at least five years, saving you the cost and trouble of repainting. Best of all, baby will have something to attract his attention. My son babbled for months in animated conversation with the stick figures on his wallpaper. For the budget minded, wallpaper need not cost a fortune. Patterns are available in all price ranges from about $4 a roll to the more costly decorator papers at $21 a roll. (See Chapter 8 for more details on wallpaper.)

For the modest sum of about $75 you could paper a room yourself of about 11′ by 13′ using an inexpensive paper. If this seems too costly or too difficult, you might elect to paper one or two walls and paint the others. A friend of mine chose a stylized giraffe wallpaper in riotous colors for the crib wall and ceiling and painted the other three walls in a hot orange to match. Since the room was small and needed something exciting at the window she had an awning made in a matching fabric and put the changing table in the closet. Infants don't need much hanging space! Her baby furniture was hand-me-downs refinished in a lacquer paint to coordinate with the wallpaper.

Another solution is to use a wallpaper border along the ceiling of the room and stick-on nursery appliques along the walls themselves. If you are artistically inclined or know someone who is, you might attempt to paint scenes on the walls themselves. (More about this in Chapters 6 and 8.)

If you decide to paint the walls and are limited in color by the landlord's requirements, you may use poster art for the same cheerful effects. Color will also play a role on the floor. You might want to install a checkerboard tile floor or an interesting tweed or patterned carpet. Stay away, though, from very restricting patterns such as a highly styled geometric. This may grow tiresome long before the floor is worn out.

BONUS NURSERY TIPS

1. Open shelves are open invitations for pint-sized room wreckers. Until the toddler can understand what "no" really means, keep the shelves out of his reach.

2. Don't put your child's table and chairs near the window or a high chest of drawers. He'll climb every mountain—and the first conquest is the table top. From there it's just a step away from the window sill or other heights and danger.

3. There are plastic plugs available at hardware stores that block electrical outlets. Buy them and use them before you have an accident.

Even the basics in nursery furniture have an individual style. *Above left*, a traditional look in chests and crib. More frills and a French influence in the nursery, *above right*. A streamlined look with a low to the floor profile, *below*.

A crib and companion pieces in red and white, *above*. The Scandinavian appeal with its natural blond wood finish, *below*, in chests and a crib that converts to a settee.

In these nurseries decorating ingenuity makes the most of limited space. *Above*, a tiny room includes all the nursery essentials plus extras such as the shelves with shades to hide storage, and fabric on the ceiling where the baby can see it. *Below*, nursery necessities fill a room with cheerful motifs that are repeated in cut-outs on the window shades. Colorful plastic bins on shelves store baby items first, toys when the child is older.

Do-it-yourself projects help keep costs down in the nursery, *above*. Among the cost cutting ideas: ready-to-finish furniture including the bookcase, rocker, and stool, the ready-stick shag carpet tiles, and sheer curtains at the cradle.

The nursery, *left*, keeps things simple with straight-lined furniture in red and white. The walls are covered with sky blue paneling, an easy-to-maintain and almost permanent installation.

Orange, pink, and olive green colors the nursery, *opposite*. This nursery will easily make the transition to toddler and teen.

The catchy combination of a plaid and a stripe come together in the nursery, *below*. In orange and brown, unorthodox colors for a nursery, the fabrics provide a background that will be suitable through teen years. For extra contrast the stripes run vertically on the window shades and horizontally on the drawers.

ROOMS TO GROW UP IN

DECORATING, FROM THREE TO ELEVEN YEARS

At the risk of being repetitive, even belaboring a point, I'd like to emphasize that "knowing your child" is the key to his room decor. It's your child who will let you know by the way he behaves when he's ready for a room change. This time will come just about when he outgrows his crib. And I don't mean this literally. Some children are content to stay put in their cribs well past their third birthday. Others are climbing over the rails after they turn one.

Whether your decision to take down the crib is arbitrary or based on necessity (another baby on the way), the collapse of the crib signals a new stage in your child's personal development. He is ready for a bed and accordingly his room should be rearranged to symbolize his new independence. This way the child will come to feel that he is getting something very special, a new room, rather than losing his security—the crib. And with minimal changes this room should fulfill your child's needs until the eleventh birthday or about the time that elementary school is over.

By three, a child is ready and often anxious to have a room designed especially for him. Plan it with his needs in mind and trust him to use it well and with respect.

These are the years when the child learns by doing—physically, emotionally, and mentally. His moods will change from day to day, his needs from month to month. But the basics stay the same. The room must be attractive, stimulating, and sturdy enough to withstand the normal wear and tear inflicted by children on the move.

When you are converting the nursery for an older child there are a number of things to consider—what you will be keeping from the nursery, what you will be discarding, and what you will be buying. The first thing you've got to change is the crib. Next you must consider the floor space since this is your child's primary play area. You will want to decide how to store his toys, what furniture to select, and which scheme to use. You might at this point draw up a list of what in the room will remain the same and what will change.

When the crib comes out you may substitute a bed—unless you already have a spare bed in the room and plan to use this one. This is the stage when some manufacturers recommend purchasing a juvenile or junior bed. This is a bed somewhat smaller than a twin equipped with sides so that the child does not fall out. In my opinion, a junior bed is an unnecessary investment. The size is a disadvantage because your child will grow out of it and the sides are needed only for a short time. These can be bought separately, used for the period of adjustment, and then stored away.

More enticing and certainly more decorative are the special juvenile beds built in the shapes of cars, boats, busses, airplanes . . . whatever the imagination conjures up. (See Chapter 9 for more information on these.) Because these beds are custom designs, usually special order, they are expensive. Some start at $300 and go up, up, and away to $1,000. Your child will find them just as exciting as you will, but buyer beware. Children's tastes are fickle and they may very well outgrow their fancy for a fancy bed. Unless you can build something yourself consider the practical.

By practical I mean a bed such as a regular twin on a frame or a captain style bed with drawers beneath. A trundle or a bunk bed will make room for overnight guests without taking up the floor space required of twin beds. A platform bed will actually free the floor—if it is built high enough with room underneath for playing. And floor space is one of the key considerations for this age group, especially from three to seven years.

The floor is your child's playground. Sitting on the floor he will build cities of blocks, paint, rest, and even picnic if weather permits. To accommodate the focus on the floor it makes sense to plan a layout with most furniture hugging the perimeter of the room leaving the center area empty for playtime. In essence this is a layout just the opposite of the conventional living room plans where most of the furniture juts into the middle of the room for the sake of aesthetics.

For the floor itself a solid patterned vinyl or dense and durable carpet is the best bet! The vinyls are obviously easier to clean and offer a flat surface—better for building and puzzle play. But a wall-to-wall carpet, synthetics particularly, does clean adequately and offers the added attraction of comfort and warmth. Scatter rugs can be a problem. Children have a tendency to trip easily and there's nothing like the edge of an area rug to fall over.

Until your child is in school he will be using his room primarily for play. Toys play a major role in your child's development but if you are not careful they will take over the room as well. You won't see the floor for the toys. All those plastic dolls, garages with their tiny plastic pieces, the blocks, the puzzles, the books. The toy chest—the most obvious catch-all for this clutter—is the least successful storage place. Once a toy is buried on the bottom it is as good as lost.

In order for your child to be able to use these toys, benefit from them, and keep a semblance of order, it's best to reorganize the toy accumulation. Start by taking the toys out of the boxes. Those colorful packages are simply a merchandising come-on. They are usually flimsy and shaped in so many different sizes that they just don't stack up.

Clear plastic containers used to keep vegetables fresh in the refrigerator are excellent for small puzzles, crayons, and toys. The larger plastic boxes used as closet organizers for shoes and shirts can house the bulkier play items such as building toys and tea sets. Don't forget that other favorite container—the coffee can. With its plastic cover that commonplace coffee can is perfect for marbles, jacks, and other collector's items. For a custom look, cover the brand name with a Con-tact print.

For the preschool years his juvenile table and chairs will be more meaningful to him for reading and writing than a desk set. A simple shelf with drawers can hold his pencils, once fitted with those plastic dividers made for silverware. At three he will need shelves for a personal library—shelves that are within his reach so that he may help himself to the books and put them back when he is finished. If shelves are not practical, try cubes of wood or plastic. If arts and crafts are an interest, a blackboard might be fun. The back of a door is an ideal spot. The door is also a fine place for showing off art. You might apply self-adhesive corkboard to the back of the door to display finger paintings, collages, and water colors in a rotating show.

At six years old when your child enters school, he still is not ready for a desk. But by eight or nine years, as a child gets into second or third grade, the focus shifts naturally from the juvenile table and chairs to a desk. The desk need not be the conventional type although that is certainly adequate. To save the expense of a desk set you might want to construct one simply by running a slab of Formica (with a drawer or two if possible) from wall-to-wall inside an alcove in the room. If there's no alcove you may be creative and run the Formica over a pair of desk height night stands or open cubes for storage. These can be replaced when the child grows older by functional file cabinets. The slab—it can be as long an 10'—provides super work surfaces. Your local lumberyard or furniture-in-the-raw store can supply you with the Formica.

Lighting in the youngster's room must also conform to the special requirements, and this means overhead lighting wherever possible. Lamps, although decorative, take up surface space and are hazardous to little children who may trip over cords and experiment with electrical plugs. If you must resort to lamps while the child is young you should make certain the cord is well hidden behind a substantial piece of furniture. When the child is older, at eight or nine years, he will need a desk lamp and a reading light over his bed. The wall mounted fixtures with extension arms are appropriate for these purposes.

THEMES AND SCHEMES

If you are starting from scratch at this age you will want a theme—or idea—around which to design the room. A source for these schemes? Look into your child's world. They are fascinated by the world around them—nature, cars, dolls, music, trucks, water, television, fashion, and even their own imaginary thoughts.

Sesame Street, that clever and educational children's television program, provides enough materials for several children's rooms. Paint the walls a bright color, perhaps Florida orange, and stencil them with king-size numbers and alphabet letters at random. The program also has many brightly colored posters that can be framed for the walls.

Automobiles and boats are naturals for youngsters' rooms and while time was when this was suitable only for boys the unisex revolution has made this, and similar themes, neutral territory.

The zoo, mother nature, the circus, animals . . . these are all worlds that your youngster is beginning to explore. You can have a lot of fun working with the idea of a "zoo" theme for the room. If the floors are wood you might paint them and stencil with paw prints. Build a cage in one corner for a collection of stuffed animals. One wall can be the wild animal area with decals of lions and tigers (or painted faces if you have the talent) and signs posted "DO NOT FEED THE MONKEYS," "BEWARE OF WILD ANIMALS," "LIONS' HOUSE CLOSED."

What if a theme is not your thing? Your child may not be interested. Perhaps your daughter is just an old-fashioned girl and wants ruffles, frills, and a canopy bed. Plan the room around the bed. With today's washable fabrics even a canopy bed can be practical. When she is older and out of the canopy stage (princess grows up) the canopy can detach and you have the basic four-poster.

Let imagination be your guide and your child's personality an inspiration. Leave lots of floor space. Plan a reading corner for the quiet times. Just keep your child in mind.

For those little ladies in your life who fancy themselves next in line to the crown, a sweet room complete with canopy bed, rocking chair, and curtains tied back with big velvet bows. By Bachstein & Lawrence.

Toy soldiers come to attention in these two children's rooms. *Top*, the soldiers keep night watch from the sentry box built into the corner of this large room. A patriotic color scheme makes sense in this setting designed by Joseph Braswell. Of special interest: a striped paper applied on the ceiling to give a tented effect. *Below*, the soldier theme takes its cue from a wallpaper border which covers the bed frame and headboard and tops off the striped walls. For a colorful bonus the closet doors are painted in contrasting colors.

Cartoon characters and juvenile television stars are
easy-to-adapt themes. Huckleberry Hound takes
center stage in the room, *above*. Sheets introduce
the character. The wall art is a clever do-it-yourself
project: it's one pillowcase split in two and framed.
The balloons were cut from multi-colored felt,
glued to the walls, and anchored with string.
Casper the Friendly Ghost, *right*, flies on the
sheets, masks, and on the kite.

Bunk or trundle beds help keep the floor free for play. *Opposite*, stacked up bunk beds and wide stripes in primary colors across the walls pick up the colors of the painted furniture.

Above, a trundle solves the problem of overnight guests without taking up floor space. The bed is white highlighted with red to coordinate with the window shades in a provincial print.

Anchors away! Bedtime should be a delight in the boy's room, *right*, which carries the nautical theme through to the bed. A striped wall covering and show-off shelf complete the picture.

There's ample room to play, *left*. On the wall a lemon yellow yardstick graphic adds interest and stretches the length of the room. Area rugs are set like stepping stones. More wall art, this time in vertical stripes and numbers, attracts attention, *below*. The furniture has a Scandinavian freshness.

There's plenty of room to grow in this young boy's room. Designer
Abbey Darer ties the colors to the tartan plaid carpet brightening
it with sunshine yellow window shades and red on the bunk beds.
When the boy turns teen the bunk beds can be replaced.

The offbeat beds are the center of attention in this trio of rooms.

Opposite top, a bed decked out with sail by sculptor Accorsi captures a youngster's imagination. Printed sheets on the sail and bed also frame the window shade.

Opposite bottom, a bed slanted on an angle is a clever compromise when both walls boast large windows treated to fanciful draperies.

Above, a new twist on the Murphy bed. The bed pulls out from the wall and swivels on a base. Designed by Gerda Clark.

Pretty yet practical, these three rooms all focus attention on the bed.

Above, designer Salvatore Cesararie frames the gingham covered bed with white wicker etageres and a matching canopy. The gingham is also shirred under the windows to conceal convenient toy storage.

In the eager pre-teener's room, *opposite top*, sleeping quarters are turned into a sitting room with a grown-up room arrangement by Abbey Darer. A tulip print splashed on the window curtains and furniture sparkles against a polka-dot print on the wall and shades.

Opposite bottom, an old iron crib had been lost and was found and recycled by designer Dorothy Baker Billings. A herd of happy pink elephants covers the walls above the chair rail with a timeless patchwork print below.

Happiness is a built-in bed, *at left*, with window seat to boot with whimsical wall plaques. Happiness is ideas in every corner, *below*. Trio of cubes on casters are casual seats and handy storage bins. Another child's delight: the bicycle basket hanging by the bed for special toys and books. To mother's delight all the fabrics are spill proof.

One print says it all in these rooms. *Above*,
designer Ruben de Saavedra keeps it simple yet
sassy with bare floors, a perky pink and white
print, a provincial bookcase, and a modern table
and chairs. *At right*, a cheerful print sets the stage
in a room by Abbey Darer. The wallpaper is
scrubbable and inexpensive. The twin bed is set
into an alcove.

A nautical theme turns an architectural problem into an asset in Bobby's room, *above*. Designer Martin Kuckly accents the structural supports for a shipshape result. The window wall plays an important design role in the room *at the left*. Vertical blinds are topped off with an awning and crossed with a wood bar with pegs for hanging hats, gloves, skates.

CHAPTER 4

FOR THE TEENAGER IN YOUR LIFE

The transition from the early years into teenage times can be, for the parent, as disruptive as a trip to the moon. Whatever was familiar in your child's behavior—his likes and dislikes—becomes foreign. While the teenager is experimenting with his personality, the parent can be undergoing a severe case of culture shock. Growing up has all of a sudden advanced at a breakneck pace pushing the speed limit.

Naturally the room that was his haven will have to undergo equally radical changes to accommodate his new interests and demands. Opposition is the word of the day. If you suggest navy walls, she'll prefer white. If you recommend a recliner, he'll say he'd rather sit on the floor. This kind of negativism is typical of the age and a clue to what to do with the room. The teenager is only trying to establish an individuality—he's trying on new independence. If successful, his room will reflect these needs.

Just what does that mean? In a word: privacy. Within the four walls the teenager should have almost everything he needs to exist like a hermit. The teenager with his erratic mood changes, values, above all, a chance to seclude himself. To talk on the telephone, alone. To listen to his records, alone and with his friends. To have a room that shows off his interests and salutes his growing maturity.

THE MAKE OVER

Once again, as the room grows with your child, the basics stay the same. You will use the same bed. The same chest of drawers. The same desk and chair. Even the shelves if you have them. But all the relics of childhood will go out the door in your teenager's quest to grow up fast.

Now the most essential and elementary difference in the room will be the layout. For the past ten or eleven years the floor has been the key for play with all the furniture up against the wall wherever possible. Now the room will take on a more mature aspect with a layout similar to other bedrooms in the house. Because the floor space is no longer as important the furniture can jut out into the room at right angles.

At this time you will also probably want to freshen up the look of the room with whatever you need to introduce sophistication and an updated decor. This may mean anything from a change in wallcovering to new bedspreads and color scheme.

SOME CHANGES TO BE MADE

What exactly does happen to the room at this age? The toys disappear—except for a few cherished souvenirs. Out goes the blackboard, the easel, the toy chest. All of these will be replaced, naturally, by equally important symbols of coming of age—the record player, the tape deck, the telephone, the hair dryer.

While storage was directed toward fighting the toy problem before, it will now become directed at taming or at least harnessing the equipment explosion. The stereo equipment usually finds its way to the best location either on the shelves or on top of the chest. Records are another problem. The best way to keep them orderly is within the confines of those plastic record sorters or racks available in department and hardware stores. At least these help to keep the records standing.

Sports equipment, if your teenager is the outdoor or active type, can run the gamut from ice skates to ski boots, from tennis rackets and baseball bats to riding crops and shoulder pads. A few of these items can be used as decorative elements. The tennis racket can be mounted right on the wall as can the bat and even the ice skates. More cumbersome items such as boots and padding would be better off stored in a mud room or up on a closet shelf.

This is also the time when pin-ups take on a special meaning. Almost everything, from a basketball game program to a ballot from the high school election, is worth saving and posting in the room. Souvenirs are collected from restaurants, rock concerts, parties, vacations. A giant bulletin board, perhaps taking up even the entire front of the closet door, will protect the walls from the scarring effects of Scotch tape.

And speaking of the closet, the inside of the door should have a full length mirror for close up inspections in privacy.

Furniture

The changes you will be making now focus on fabrics—perhaps floor and wall coverings—a few pices of furniture and accessories. You will want to qualify all your decisions about what to buy with the fact that teenagers are not neat. Nor are they careful. Nor are they cautious. While a few of them are more respectful about personal property than others, this generally is not the age of good housekeeping. This observation translated into buyer tips means shopping for durability.

The comfortable chair that left the nursery comes back here perhaps with an ottoman for comfortable studying, reading, or relaxing. Your teenager will sit in it sometimes, flop in it other times. Eat in it. Drink there and never remember to take off his shoes. So how about a washable vinyl upholstery for your sanity and his. Even a slipcover of washable fabric will be an advantage now.

At thirteen with junior high school requirements and a steadily increasing homework load the desk takes on much more significance.

A big work surface is a big benefit for the desk. There should be room for a typewriter, telephone (if you allow your teenager that privilege), and space to spare for writing reports. A Formica surface will protect the desk from the stains of soda cans and other spills. An alternative cover-up is a glass or better yet a Plexiglas top cut to fit. Books, of course, can easily be set up on shelves, either freestanding etageres or wall bracketed types.

DECORATING THE ROOM

Planning to redecorate your teenager's room now? Act as a professional would—to the best of your emotional ability. Treat the teenager as the client you are working to please. This is not meant to sound ingratiating or permissive. A teenager, as you probably already know, has an opinion on everything. It is his room you are working with. And even though it is your money, the results should please him first, you second. This goes from color choice down the line to furniture selection. What good will it do if you order a chair that you like but that is not comfortable or appealing to him?

During the years from twelve to eighteen a teenager's taste will develop with his development. In the early teens when sexual identity is very important, the room may well put a temporary emphasis on those elusive qualities of femininity or masculinity. From sixteen years on with college looming ahead there is a breaking away from home and the room will mirror this change also.

How do you show off these personality changes in the room design? The bulletin board is a visible display area. The book shelves also provide an obvious location for collections and souvenirs. Poster art can be rotated to reflect changing interests. Accessories such as throw pillows, decorative mirrors, or even sculpture, can be interchanged. As your teenager voices excitement in a new hobby or school study help him bring this interest into the room. If it's photography or painting, frame the art work and hang it. Geology? Begin a rock collection and display it well. Politics? Stick the buttons, bumper stickers, posters, flyers, all up on a specially framed corkboard.

The raison d'etre of the room, the bed itself,

can redefine the room. A new bedspread immediately freshens up the setting. More dramatic and involved is an entire new look for the bed. Put it up on an elevated platform about a foot off the floor, carpeting the platform to match the rest of the flooring in the room. Or, as the teenager spends more and more time away from home, replace the mattress and boxspring with a sleep sofa.

The color scheme will also evolve now into a more subtle and sophisticated relationship. There is less of a need for vivid jarring tones. The navy, orange, white contrasts of the past might mutate into navy and beige with soft orange accents. Apple green, yellow, and white become tree green, sand, and cocoa brown.

BONUS TEENAGE TIPS

1. Encourage neatness by providing a place for everything so that everything may someday be in its place.

2. A lot of the paraphernalia that is ordinarily bathroom bound will find its way into the teenager's room. This includes make-up, medicine for skin problems, hair dryers, curlers, hand mirrors. Those very same plastic boxes that worked wonders as toy organizers in the toddler's room will do the job here.

3. A light at the head of the bed becomes important as reading and studying in bed becomes a habit. This may be the customary night table and lamp or a more practical wall mounted light on an extension arm.

A pair of rooms in tune with the teenager's time is practical as well as attractive. *Above*, a classic contemporary room designed by Gerda Clark for Abraham & Straus features an easy-to-make bed and a collection of posters. Circles, stripes, and sports equipment give a superstar appeal to the room, *left*. The moderately priced furniture creates a functional study area with room for collections.

A special study area makes homework more palatable for teens. *Opposite top*, window alcove makes a convenient corner for desk and chair. Desk area is centered between campaign style chests in the bedroom, *opposite bottom*, designed by Jane Victor.

Windows which might have been a problem, *left*, become a benefit. To help the windows make the turn structured by the Victorian architecture, plaid curtains and coordinated window shades follow the curves.

Below, boys bunk together in a room with the flavor of the Wild West. The blanket-covered beds are framed with paneling.

Easy-care room, *right*, with ample shelf space uses an autumn-hued plaid for its scheme.
Below, a rustic room wraps it up for a budding folk singer.

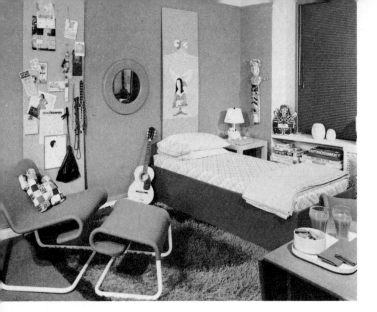

Wall space is as important to teenagers as floor space was to the toddler.

Top left, a pair of felt-covered bulletin boards hold urgent social notices. Vibrant colors range from bright red to deep purple in the chair and ottoman. Record album covers, *center*, combine art and music appreciation for a unique wall arrangement. Knotty pine walls in the room, *bottom left*, provide hanging for hats, art, sports equipment.

Opposite, a teen's very special collection of Indian artifacts is displayed in well-lit shadow boxes built into units flanking the bed. A striped fabric in colors typical of the Southwest covers bed and windows. For instructions on making display cabinets, see page 123.

Here are three different answers to the same problem—where to put twin beds.

Opposite, two beds rest their heads on the same wall.

Below, they come together at a right angle with a cube in between.

Right, the beds line up with the odd angles of the walls.

Designed to take a teen right through the college years, this charming attic retreat, *opposite*, takes its scheme from the spring bouquets on the wallpaper and matching fabric. Pink tulips grow in the room, *right*, designed by Barbara Skouras. The flowers bloom everywhere from the laminated window shades to the sprouting finials on the poster bed.

Family hand-me-downs are put to special use in the young lady's room, *below*. Fresh white paint gives new life to the armoire, wicker desk and chair, and old iron and brass bed. By Gerda Clark for Abraham & Straus.

The crown canopy has two interpretations here. *Left*, designer David Barrett crowns the bed flush against the wall in a lollypop print used throughout the room. *Right*, Jane Victor hangs the crown directly over the bed and drapes the panels down to the bed posts.

CHAPTER 5

THE RACE FOR SPACE

It's often double or nothing when it comes to planning the room for the younger set. The race for space, when it comes down to a very personal level in your home, will mean one of two things. Either your youngster's room is smaller than small and relies on your imagination to stretch its limits. Or you must divide and conquer, putting two or more children in the same bedroom.

In approaching the problem of how to make the most of what you have, the solution comes in two parts—illusion and reality. First is using design to create the illusion of more space. Second is making realistic use of what actually exists—all six surfaces: the floor, four walls, and ceiling.

Design can be used to many advantages besides the obvious end of making a room attractive and exciting. Properly applied good design may seemingly push out the walls. You can stretch space with your choice of color and pattern as well as with layout.

Light, muted or cool colors are categorized by designers as receding tones. They seem to fade away into the background and in doing so increase the illusion of space to spare. Bright, warm colors work just the opposite effect. They advance, attract attention and correspondingly shrink the dimensions of a room.

What are the receding colors? As simply as possible they are as much a question of intensity as of tone. A very pale red might be a receding color while a vivid red would definitely be an advancing tone. In general the receding colors are the cooler, lighter shades such as pastels, beiges, muted yellows, blues. Since color is such an important ingredient in the child's room, if the size of the room indicates the use of the receding tones while the child's age suggest more vivid colors you can compromise.

Use the muted colors as background including the more exciting hues as accents and pick-ups in the room. For example you might plan a toddler's room in pale yellow and white accented with trims of intense purple (believe it or not, children love purple). If the room is sky blue bring some life in with hot pink, acid green, Florida orange.

Patterns may also work to expand or shrink the room. A vertical stripe lifts the ceiling while a horizontal stripe wrapped around the same room would trigger claustrophobia. Too much pattern in a room may constrict it. The patterns competing for attention will confuse the eye and break up the continuity of the room. This is applicable to pattern on the floor as well as the walls. If the room is small it makes more sense from a decorative point of view to use either a solid or a tiny repeat pattern. No busy checks or plaids here, please.

Wall-to-wall carpeting pushes out the perimeters of the room as does linoleum or vinyl tile. Area rugs do just the opposite. A rug here and there gives a spotty impression, again breaking up the continuity of floor space.

The second way to make the most of the space you have is to make realistic use of what actually exists—all six surfaces. This will necessitate paying careful attention to the layout. The most prominent and important piece of furniture in the room is the bed. There are a number of inventive and practical ways to increase the sleeping quarters without infringing on the floor space.

With only one child in the room a trundle bed is a great problem solver. The occasional overnight guest can be easily accommodated by pulling out the extra bed. A trundle is just not as practical for children sharing a room. The space it takes up is minimal but the inconvenience of pulling it out every night and the problem of walking around it cancel the benefits. For doubling up, the bunk bed is the most logical and reasonable solution in a tiny room. Although you may have to referee a battle for the bunks (who sleeps on top is a constant source of competition) it does stack up as a space saver.

Another solution in a tiny room is that old standby, the Murphy bed. This bed, designed to pull out of the wall or closet, leaves the floor virtually empty during the day. There are many styles of the Murphy bed on the market, some handsomely fitted into wall units complete with drawers and shelves.

When there is space to spare in the room but children still double up, twin beds are both convenient and comfortable. One of the best ways to arrange a room with twin beds is to place them at right angles to each other in a corner with either a night table or a cube dividing them. You might even consider having a custom corner unit built that will permit the bed to slide under it. Twin beds jutting out into the room take up no more actual floor space in terms of square footage than those lined up against the wall. But they look like they do and illusion is a good part of the game.

You may also customize your beds if you have the budget or the talent. Build them up on stilts. Frame them into an alcove in the room. Build them into the wall. (More on this in Chapter 9.)

Make the walls work for your child also. The wall surface is an ideal divider. You may use it to set off separate sleeping areas or to distinguish work and play places. In a room that sisters share, for example, you might mount a strip of corkboard across the length of the room with a strip running vertically up and down the wall separating the beds. Or you might mount a curtain on a ceiling track to close in the bed at night. For a more permanent solution, construct an actual divider extending from the existing wall to isolate a study corner. Remember, though, this may make the room appear much smaller because the divider will stop the eye's movement.

In a small room utilize wall space to substitute for the lack of floor space. Mount your shelves on the wall. Hang the dresser on the wall. You might even consider cantilevering a writing surface or desk from the wall (if the wall is strong enough) to keep the floor free.

A good deal of the race for space relies on clever design planning. When you have the option to choose, always choose light, airy looking furniture for this small room. Use a wicker chair rather than a heavy vinyl recliner. See-through pieces such as plexiglass tables will increase the illusion of more space. Pay careful attention to the window treatment. In a small room you will not want an overpowering window that will call undue attention to itself and make it stand out. A simple shade would be more suitable than a fussy drapery treatment.

Look to the ceiling for some help. Use overhead lighting to free the furniture from this burden. Paint the ceiling a light color to give it a lift.

Bunk beds with a difference promote peaceful
co-existence for sisters in less than ample space.
The ruffled curtains are made from sheeting.

The Murphy bed, that old standby, gets a new look
in the teenager's room, *right*. Pastel stripes perk up
the room in a puckered print.

Space solvers for doubling up at bedtime include, *at left*, beds placed foot to foot along the wall and separated by a bulletin board. *Below*, what looks like a trunk offers two surprises. On the right the bottom drawer rolls out on casters; on the left the bed slides out to rest on fold-down legs. In the boy's room, *opposite*, designer T. Miles Gray tailors the layout to suit a trundle bed.

Built-ins solve the space race in this room designed with a pair of active youngsters in mind. A loft bed built for two stretches across the width of the room housing a desk and storage space beneath. The other walls are covered with blackboard composition for an always changing art show. The table opens to make an extra bed. Both rooms on these pages by Gerda Clark for Abraham & Straus.

There's room for three in the bedroom, *above*. The newborn sleeps in an antique steel crib while the older sisters have their own end of the room with beds that can stack up to a bunk arrangement. The wall unit is decorated with folk art motifs to amuse both baby and sisters. Painted on the floor is that generation spanner—the hopscotch board.

The circus comes to town, *left*. Clowns and other circus motifs decorate the sheets and sleeping bags on the sturdy bunk bed of red tubing.

Below, a drapery on a ceiling track can be closed to divide the room in two when privacy is more important than companionship.

BUDGET STRETCHERS

In decorating, money (specifically, the lack of it) is the biggest headache. Happily, in furnishing your child's room a tight budget is not as great a handicap. Ingenuity, do-it-yourself projects, and the impact of bright colors work together to make up for whatever money can't buy.

As a matter of fact, while in other rooms budget projects may have a makeshift quality that doesn't live up to the intended image, in the children's room the inexpensive items not only save, they also make sense. These projects give you and your family a chance to work together. And they have the added benefit of being geared to your child's immediate needs. Because there is no great expense involved, when the needs change the items can be discarded or refinished.

In planning your budget, the challenge comes in balancing two figures—what you have to spend and what you assume it will cost. To figure out what the costs will be for the room you should refer back to your child's room chart (Chapter 1).

1. Itemize the cost of all essential purchases, such as the bed, desk, chair, etc.

2. Shop around making certain that the price you have gotten is the best possible price, taking into account both quality and durability.

3. Subtract the amount you must spend from the amount you can spend. The end figure will let you know just how much you will have left over to buy other things such as floor covering, window and wall treatment, bedspreads, accessories.

Following this order will help you avoid frustrating and costly mistakes. And it should keep you from impulsively spending most of your budget on relatively frivolous items, such as wallpaper, leaving little for more important purchases, such as a bed and chair. Remember also in planning your budget that it doesn't pay to skimp on purchases that are meant to last, such as mattresses, chests, carpeting.

Now you are ready to begin with budget decorating ideas for the entire room—walls, floor, furniture, and windows.

HOW TO SAVE WITH SHEETS

One of the bonanzas of the colorful sheet revolution is the linens' surprise success as a decorating delight. When sheets exchanged their conservative solids for imaginative patterns they left the bed far behind. In children's rooms sheeting used instead of more costly fabrics is appropriate and practical precisely because they are sheets and therefore washable.

Sheets are making it big all over the room. They can be shirred on the walls. Quilted as bedspreads. Hung as canopies. Draped at the windows. Sheets can turn plain into fancy with a minimum expense and a maximum impact.

On the bed itself the sheets make an exciting impression just showing off their colors or stitched up as bed throw or matching spread and dust ruffle.

A number of pattern companies have easy sew-it-yourself instructions geared to working with sheets for such projects. For a somewhat more complicated but obviously terrific result you might make a ceiling hung bed canopy or panels and draperies for a four poster.

On the walls you may opt either to cover up as you would with wallpaper or shirr the sheets for a softer effect. To cover up the walls cut the sheet to desired size, apply with wallpaper paste and stretch tightly to avoid wrinkles. Accomplish the same look with a different method by using a staple gun to hang the sheet mounted on molding strips and stretched to the floor. Shirring sheets makes decorative sense in two situations: one, when you will want to remove them for occasional washing, and two, when the walls are badly cracked or layered with years and years of wallpaper pile-ons.

To make shirred wallcoverings follow these simple instructions:

1. The shirred effect is created easily by stretching lengths of sheeting floor to ceiling shirred on narrow rods. Generally the rods are placed where the floor and the wall meet and where the ceiling and the wall meet.

2. To determine the amount of sheeting needed, measure the rod to rod height of each ceiling area separately. Add 4″ to each of these measurements as an allowance for rod pockets. The width of fabric to cover each wall or ceiling area should be approximately two times the actual width of the wall or ceiling section to allow ample shirring.

3. Any vertical seams necessary for a wall area

should be sewn at this time. Once all sheeting is cut to fit the various areas, it is time to make the rod pockets. To form rod pockets for the floor rods, merely turn under the raw edges ½″. Next, fold up an additional 1½″ hem which should be machine sewn in place to form the rod pockets. (Note: the rod pocket may be smaller, depending upon the diameter of the rod used.)

If you are planning these or any other of the sheeting home sewing projects in Chapter 11, note these helpful sewing hints:

1. Make all seams ½″.
2. Cut, never tear, the fabric.
3. Use pinking shears whenever possible.
4. When the sheet pattern runs in one direction only you may need a larger size sheet than specified to work with the pattern.

WAYS TO SAVE ON THE FLOOR

You may be longing for a deep shag running wall-to-wall in the kid's quarters but you know that the price is out of sight. After all, a good carpet with eight to ten years of life in it will cost anywhere from $10 a yard up. Even for a small room (10′ by 12′) that means an expense of $135. You could hunt for a bargain (let's say at $6 a yard) but chances are that the carpet will be unsightly within a year.

You could substitute vinyl or linoleum (see more about these floor coverings in Chapter 8) but they are not cheap by any means. Or you might make do with remnants or with carpet tiles. But paint may be your answer.

Here, the power of the paint brush can transform an ugly duckling wood floor, if not into a beautiful swan, then at least into an amusing on-the-floor game area or focal point for interest. All you need are the wood floors, imagination, and the appropriate paint. Your local paint or hardware store dealer can recommend which paint and sealer will work best for you.

If the floors are in decent repair you can refresh them with a bright coat of paint.

To paint your floor:

1. Remove all wax and dirt.
2. Fill in any cracks.
3. Use a roller to apply paint, first outlining the perimeter around the baseboard with a smaller brush so that you do not stain the moldings.
4. Be sure that each paint application is dry before applying another.

If you are talented enough at free hand art you might execute your own original art at this point. Let's say you painted the floor chrome yellow. Pink, purple, tangerine, and white posies with apple green stems scattered randomly across the floor make a very pretty picture.

For the not-so-sure artist, the old art of stenciling is just as effective. You may opt to cut your own stencil perhaps to match a print in the room or to express your own originality. Or you may buy a stencil precut. To stencil your floor:

1. Trace your design on stencil paper. (Available at art supply stores.) There should be a separate stencil for each color in your pattern.
2. Cut out the stencil with a very sharp knife. If the edges are ragged the stencil will be also.
3. Tape your stencil to the floor with masking tape after you have practiced with this or another stencil to master the technique. Try it out on either cardboard or brown paper.
4. Paint with a stencil brush in dabbing strokes. You might ask your art store dealer to recommend which paint to use. If the paint is too thin it will run out under the stencil.
5. Use a sealer after the art work is dry to protect the pattern.

You might repeat the stencil motif on an occasional piece of furniture in the room or on a window shade.

If carpet is a must a budget special is a patchwork of carpet remnant squares. These squares are cut from larger pieces and are easy to buy at special sales. Use as many different colors and patterns as you like and apply them to the floor with glue or double face tape. A word of caution: try to assemble pieces of similar textures, either all shags, all velvets, or all low pile. It will give the final patchwork a sense of consistency if they blend in texture.

WAYS TO SAVE ON THE WALLS

In your youngster's room the four walls that define his private world have a special significance. They are not only the best but also the most visible place for a color explosion. A vinyl finish wallpaper is a very basic and effective way to introduce color into the room (see more about wallpaper in Chapter 8), but it may not balance with your budget, especially with the price of a wallpaper hanger tacked on. Again, paint is the cheapest and most effective alternative. With the infinite possibilities of the medium, paint is a great plus.

To paint your walls:

1. Patch up all cracks, nail holes, etc.
2. Clean the surface. If there is wallpaper, remove it.
3. Using a brush or a roller, paint from ceiling to floor. Ask your paint dealer for special instructions if you are using unusual paint or if your climate is a problem.

Paint your walls all the same color. Paint two in red and two in yellow. Paint each a different tone—orange, pink, apple green, and yellow. A semigloss or enamel finish is shinier and therefore more exciting in a child's room.

Graphics, super or otherwise, on the walls will accomplish the same end for the room as wallpaper or art. The graphics will bring to the room pattern and pizzazz all at a minimum cost.

Another benefit of graphics is that they can be scaled up or down to conform to the size of your room. Depending on the age and inclination of your child the graphics can be anything from hard edge geometrics to swirling circles or simple rainbows. To paint your own graphic decide first on a design and color scheme. In one child's room a talented young designer painted a king-sized Indian motif borrowed from a pattern in a Navaho rug. In her other youngster's room she painted a rising sun breaking through layers of multicolored clouds.

Sketch your design on a piece of extra large graph or grid paper, as it is called, scaled to the size of the room. Next, transfer the design to the painted wall surface in a pencil outline. Using masking tape to keep the lines straight, paint it in. Here, again, you will want a semigloss paint. Have a trial run first. You will have to learn how to keep the paint from dripping and the wall is no place to practice.

You may actually decide to paint on a headboard instead of buying the real thing. This could be a design right at the head of the bed such as a super-sized daisy, or a *trompe l'oeil* headboard, or a calendar of your child's birthday month.

WAYS TO SAVE ON FURNITURE

As I wrote before and here again for emphasis, it never pays to skimp on quality. You can nevertheless manage to buy durable, good quality furniture without spending a fortune. A popular and successful way to save is with unpainted furniture available in a variety of styles. As long as it is well built this furniture will last through your youngster's growing years and even past. While he grows you can paint, repaint, and paint it once more to change the room's appearance. For a more customized touch, change the drawer pulls using alphabet blocks for the nursery years, ball or flower pulls at the next stage, and more sophisticated Lucite or brass hardware for teens.

There are plenty of accent pieces that you can build yourself, from the most elementary projects to more advanced carpentry works.

1. Make a cube seat with a top on hinges. Put it on casters so it can be easily moved about the room. It doubles up as a storage piece.

2. Do you have an eve or dormer in the room? Take advantage of the sloping ceiling to construct a doll's house, garage, or fire station.

3. Use a carpet tube to make a low seat covered up with carpet leftovers.

4. Make a desk with two ingredients. Buy a flat surface stock door and mount it on saw horses or file cabinets.

5. Searching for an unusual headboard? Try an old heavily carved door. Or a trellis with mirrored Plexiglas mounted behind it.

6. Upholster a Parsons table in a fabric to match the room.

WAYS TO SAVE ON WINDOWS

In a well dressed room the window treatment deserves its name. The window is literally treated to a very special, often custom order, drapery and valance suitable in period and style to the furnishings in the room. As you can imagine and probably have found out this costs a lot of money. Fortunately this pretension is not appropriate in the child's room.

Making your own window curtains will be an enormous savings. In a sheeted room you might sew cafe curtains to match the print in the room or do the same with short tie-back ruffled curtains.

A very simple solution might be to build your own valance in a simple box or scalloped form and upholster this with a coordinated fabric. A window shade pulling down under the valance will permit privacy and may be either in a pattern, solid, or laminated to match. There are simple kits available to laminate-your-own-shades. Incidentally, fabric, not wallpaper, is recommended for laminating. The other tears and curls at the edges.

Save with sheets. *Above*, three sheeting patterns
—a stripe, plaid, and floral—spruce up the room.
Right, a striped sheeting covers all including the
walls.

Keep costs down with clever, pretty ideas for a little girl's room.
Abbey Darer shows how: paint an old camp trunk to store blankets
or toys; build a doll's house under an eave; use a sewing machine
base as a desk; sew it all yourself from window curtains to
polka-dot spread.

The bed is an engaging focal point here. An unpainted piece of
furniture in its first life, the plaid-patterned bed was a
do-it-yourself project with a little help from masking tape to keep
the lines straight. By Gerda Clark for Abraham & Straus.

Save on furniture . . . *opposite top left*, school desks reclaimed from the junk pile get new life with a little sanding and a fresh coat of paint. Save on walls . . . with a painted mural of Smokey the Bear, *opposite top right*, and with self-adhesive paper on the walls, bed, and shelves, *opposite bottom*.

Save on walls . . . *above*, with a simple, inexpensive train mural on a scrubbable wallcovering.

Simple comic-strip sheets are enough to bring color and excitement to the room, *left*. The walls, painted in bright red and yellow, repeat the comic-strip color and the door becomes a pin-up gallery for pillowcases.

Build a bedroom with separate but equal quarters. The whole project can be put together by the home carpenter (see page 119 for directions) and decorated with sheets promoting the sporting life.

A quick, easy project separates sleeping and working quarters in a smaller than small room. Floor to ceiling carpet tubes painted red, white, blue create this see-through divider.

More budget ideas to imitate!

Above, a curtain rod hung at the child's height holds bicycle baskets for easy storage. Easy-to-build shelves are close to the floor, perfect for easy access.

Top left, a wallpaper border at the ceiling brings color and pattern to a room without the cost of papering the entire space.

Left, a jungle spread introduces a safari theme carried out with tent and monkey bars for little swingers.

CHAPTER 7

CRIBBING FROM THE EXPERTS

Watching a room grow with a child, actually visualizing the changes, is the best way to illustrate the basic belief of this book—that you can plan ahead to have a continuity of design and therefore buy wisely to save time, money, and energy.

Here we have the work of three top interior designers to show just how this concept works with sketches of a room in the process of growing up—Stage 1, the nursery; Stage 2, from three to eleven years; Stage 3, teenage. In these renderings and photographs you will see for yourself just what changes in the room and what stays the same.

RUBEN DE SAAVEDRA

Mr. de Saavedra presents a plan for a growing boy living in an apartment house. He sets the stage with a nursery in red, white, and blue, because it is a safe scheme that almost everybody finds appealing. He has combined a practical and simple layout with a basic background design that changes only when it must.

Stage 1, nursery:

COLOR SCHEME: Red, white, and blue with blue dominating the tri-color scheme.

FLOOR: Wood painted an off white and stenciled in a large Mondrian plaid to introduce pattern and color and to define the furniture placement.

WALLS: Covered in a textured white vinyl for a crisp clean look.

CEILING: White.

WINDOW: A mother's concern here is for safety. The designer makes the windows safe with a shutter treatment, double louvres that lock from the inside. The shutters are painted white with red knobs. A surface for play runs underneath the window providing space beneath for toy storage.

BABY FURNITURE: A crib in white with blue trim. A

changing table, not shown, but on the wall as you walk into the room. Chest is hand-me-down painted white with blue trim.

FOR MOTHER: A wicker rocker and pull up bench. Also, an extra bed for those times when baby is sick.

The bed is covered in a red, white, and blue tweed with bolsters in terry cloth that can be easily washed.

LIGHTING: Plastic overhead fixture that cannot be broken by bouncing balls and flying toys.

ART: Quilt over extra bed and poster over chest.

Stage 2, from three to eleven years:

COLORS: The same.

FLOOR: It can remain in the Mondrian pattern or be repainted in a stripe as in the sketch.

WALLS: The same vinyl.

WINDOW: Treatment the same although two chairs have been added for homework on this shelf surface.

FURNITURE: Here is where change occurs. The crib goes out and is replaced by a day bed with the chest opposite. A bulletin board goes up over the chest and a poster or painting over the day bed.

Stage 3, teenage:

LAYOUT: The designer has reversed the entire room for the sake of change, although this is not essential.

COLOR SCHEME: Changes to sand, gray, and brown.

WALLS: Painted sand color.

WINDOW: Shutters stripped to natural wood with Lucite knobs.

FLOOR; Low pile commercial carpet in colors of room.

FURNITURE: Bed is covered in a print in shades of brown, gray, and beige. A club chair is upholstered in a matching fabric. The shelf still functions but a more formal desk is added at head of the bed. On the opposite wall shelves are put up over a chest for clothing.

LIGHTING: Track lights ceiling with wall mounting lights on either side of bed.

ART: Photos of friends and family are framed in clear plastic and hung on walls in addition to posters.

JANE VICTOR

Jane Victor, a designer with a very strong sense of color, here sets up a room suitable for either a boy or a girl. All through the stages she uses unorthodox but definitely exciting colors with a scheme built around purple, a favorite shade of most little ones.

Stage 1, nursery:

LAYOUT: The scene has been set for the growing child with all the nursery necessities and the basic color scheme.

COLOR SCHEME: Purple and shades of that hue, white, blue, beige.

FLOOR: Painted in the room's colors in concentric rectangles.

WALLS: In this setting the walls have much of the design interest with a fabric stretched or shirred all around the room. On the window wall an undulating print by Riverdale has been applied to sliding panels that open to set light in. The corners of the room have been cut with angular panels upholstered in purple and decorated with novel pocket-style bags to hold toys and extras. All fabric here of Celanese Fortrel.

BABY FURNITURE: A crib sprayed purple to match, a chest of drawers painted beige and topped with a pad to double as a changing table.

FOR MOTHER: A daybed and rocker.

Stage 2, from three to eleven years:

LAYOUT: The room has grown up on two walls.
While the daybed remains on the opposite side (not
shown), the chests now support an extra walk-up bed
and the left wall features a suspended desk.

COLOR SCHEME: The same.

FLOOR: The same with extra pillows added for floor
seating.

WALLS: The fabric has been removed on two walls
and the walls painted. The print remains on the
panels.

84

Photographs courtesy of Celanese Corporation with
fabrics of Fortrel and cotton.

Stage 3, teenage:

LAYOUT: Those adaptable chests have moved again. This time they've parted company and flank the bed which has moved back to the center of its original wall. The chests are topped off with a construction of giant tinker toys used to show off hobby materials.

WALLS: The left and center walls have been upholstered with a plaid by Lanscot-Arlen of Celanese Fortrel and cotton.

FURNITURE: A hammock is the most prominent and relaxing addition.

BEBE WINKLER

For a client with a young daughter, designer Bebe Winkler plans a room suitable to a house in the suburbs. In the nursery the scheme is spanking white with primary accents in red, yellow, and blue. The colors evolve to a more sophisticated range as the girl grows up. Watch the Dracaena plant grow as well.

Stage 1, nursery:

COLOR SCHEME: White with primary accents.
FLOOR: A diagonal stripe floor made up of vinyl 12″ tiles. The majority of the tiles are white. The narrow chrome yellow stripe frames in the wider lipstick red stripe.
WALLS: White.
WINDOW: White shutters.
BABY FURNITURE: Crib with tri-color panels at both ends. A changing table and chest of white wicker. Just barely seen behind the crib is another, more durable, chest in white which will remain in the room.
FOR MOTHER: A comfortable chair for feeding with a

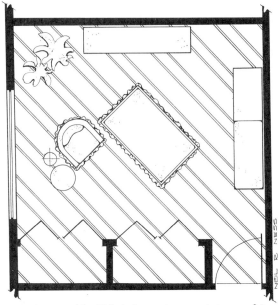

convenient table. Fabric in a primary print on a white ground to match the skirt on the crib.
LIGHTING: Overhead with exception of floor lamp for mother which will be removed when child begins to crawl.
ART: King-sized floral prints framed in bright red and yellow wood.

Stage 2, from three to eleven years:

COLOR SCHEME: The colors soften to a muted scheme with beige, white, pink, yellow, and orange.

FLOOR: Tiles covered up with an acrylic low pile "strawberries and cream" pink carpet.

WALLS: Wallpapered to match fabric in room—a beige window pane on a white ground strewn with delicate pink, orange, and yellow posies.

WINDOW: The same.

FURNITURE: A basic box spring and mattress replaces the crib and is covered with a spread to match the wallpaper. An inexpensive wicker headboard coordinates with the rest of the wicker in the room—the desk chair and the night table. The chest comes out from behind the crib and goes on the right wall topped off with matching shelves. A basic Parsons table with drawers becomes the desk.

LIGHTING: Two white lamps with beige shades are added.

Stage 3, teenage:

COLORS: Emphasize the pink and white dropping the other accents.

FLOOR: Same carpet.

WALLS: Painted shiny white.

WINDOW: Same.

FURNITURE: Molded white plastic furniture accessories in a very modern room. The bed is turned flush against the wall and covered with a quilted sailcloth in white vinylized for protection and stitched in pink for accent. The lamps stay the same but get shiny white shades.

8

WHAT TO DO WITH YOUR FLOOR, WINDOWS, WALLS,

Today's dependence on technology has even invaded the aesthetic world of decorating. Time was when a carpet meant wall-to-wall wool. Wallpaper was paper and had to be put up by a professional. Windows were covered with draperies, curtains, or shades. That was that.

Well, times do change and the consumer is caught in the middle of a decorating world dependent on jargon, technological terms, and infinite though usually discernible differences between products.

A project as simple as carpeting a room has become complex. Do you still want wool if you can afford it? Or would one of the synthetics or a blend be better? If so, which synthetic will suit your purpose—acrylic, polyester, nylon, or polypropylene olefin? What construction is best? Woven, knitted, tufted? And just to make it a little more difficult—what about padding?

You'll fare no better at the wallpaper store. Do you want a vinyl, prepasted and pretrimmed, or would a grasscloth be more suitable? How about a strippable?

To help you make some sense out of this "professional tech-talk" let's digest the terms from the floor up.

THE GREAT FLOOR COVER-UPS

You say you want to cover-up the floor in your children's room. The wood either isn't attractive enough to show off or there is no wood base at all. What you will choose depends once again on the way your child's room will function and your personal preferences. Although there are innumerable alternatives some are not appropriate. Enamel tiles, marble, stone, and slate have no place in a child's room. You will probably opt for either a smooth surface flooring (sheet goods such as linoleum, or vinyl tiles) or a soft floor covering (rugs, carpeting).

Choosing between the two categories involves a number of considerations. Ask yourself:

1. Will we be staying in this home or moving soon?

2. Which flooring is easier for me to maintain?

3. What is better for my child?

Obviously, if you are moving there is no sense in installing a costly floor that cannot be taken with you. If you are planning to live in your home for many years you will want to decide which flooring is more convenient for you. Some prefer wiping and mopping to vacuuming, and vice versa. The difference in cost between installing a wall-to-wall carpet and a vinyl can be almost insignificant.

THE FACTS ABOUT CARPET

Carpet is now available in a variety of different man-made fibers and blends of these fibers, each distinguished by a particular company brandname and each with qualities characteristic of that fiber. Wool remains the most expensive and still the most exclusive.

ACRYLIC: This fiber comes in a bevy of color choices and is similar to wool in appearance although stronger than the natural product. The carpet cleans easily, keeps its color, and doesn't pill.

NYLON: This, the most familiar fiber, is also the most durable. It comes in a wide range of colors, cleans easily, although it doesn't pill.

POLYESTER: Close to wool in looks, this fiber is durable but it does stain.

POLYPROPYLENE OLEFIN: Similar to nylon, easy to clean, and used mainly for indoor-outdoor carpeting because of its stain resistent quality.

Because carpeting is a major investment you will want to purchase it from a reliable dealer. The dealer will be responsible for installing the carpet as well as guaranteeing its wear. Carpeting generally is installed with a padding underneath. This padding works like a boxspring—it cushions, softens the feel, and increases the life of the carpet. There are a variety of paddings available, from foam rubber to all hair. The appropriate padding for your carpet will be recommended by the dealer.

Quoted prices for the carpeting should include the cost of padding and the labor charge for installation. Incidentally, there are carpets available that come bonded to a padding such as latex foam rubber and for these no extra padding is necessary.

The cost of your carpeting will depend on the size of the room and the quality of the carpet. Carpet costs are quoted by the square yard. To figure out what carpeting would cost in a room 10′ by 12′ multiply these dimensions to get 120 square feet. Divide by 9 (square yard) for 13⅓ square yards. If the carpet costs $13 a square yard your carpet will come to $174. The leftover carpeting after installation can be used to cover the closet floors.

There is a budget compromise available if carpet is too costly yet the only solution for your flooring. Carpet tiles, usually latex foam rubber backed and self-installable, come in squares in a variety of styles and colors.

ALL ABOUT SMOOTH SURFACE FLOORING

Your choices in this category are just as confusing. Vinyl, rubber, linoleum, asphalt, and cork are the alternatives. You may buy them either by the yard as sheet goods or in precut tiles. Generally the tiles are easier to install, especially for do-it-yourselfers, and have the added advantage of being individually easy to repair or replace if necessary.

Of all these floorings, *vinyl*, the most costly and the most highly styled, is also the most popular. Vinyl has become a fashion leader. The possibilities are limited only by budget. You may simply install a colorful tile wall-to-wall for an effect similar to carpet. Or you may gravitate toward one of the vinyls in look-alike patterns designed to pass for brick, ceramic, even wood. A word of warning here. If you do want one of these be sure that the grouting (the area in the tile made to resemble mortar as you would find between bricks) is not too deep. This space is a catch-all for dirt and little pieces of paper that accumulate in children's play.

Vinyl's greatest trait is its flexibility. With vinyl you can create a floor with an original twist.

You might install a vinyl checkerboard in the middle of a solid vinyl floor. Or cut it in strips of different colors to be used as raceways, landing strips, hopscotch board, or simply designs.

RUBBER: Not as stylish as vinyl but still popular.

CORK: Often used to imitate wood. A handsome flooring but not recommended because it is very porous.

LINOLEUM: Inexpensive and very durable. Not as highly styled as vinyl but fine for installations such as stripes.

ASPHALT: The least expensive and durable. It does not reduce sound and comes in a limited color range.

VINYL-ASBESTOS: Growing in popularity. Durable and easy to maintain. Available in textures but not too many colors.

Your local flooring dealer will help you select the tile most suitable to your situation considering the climate and the room itself. Below-ground rooms, for instance, will have different requirements for tiling than above-grade levels.

WHAT ABOUT WINDOWS

Window, window on the wall, I don't know what to do with you at all!

For some reason this see-through rectangle is a decorating deadend. Even after the entire room is completed the window often remains unfinished—a picture without a frame. It doesn't have to be this way if you keep a persepective. The window is meant to function. First to let in air and light. Second to provide a view—if there is one. Third, to enhance the decor.

To interpret this in decorating terms, you must provide a window treatment that will let in air and light, show off a view, and, conversely, cover-up for privacy's sake and block out the light when necessary. A tough order?

Yes and no. Starting with the black-out problem you have only a few possibilities. Venetian or slender-slatted blinds, opaque window shades, vertical blinds, and shutters will keep out most of the light. Of these only the Venetian blinds have a solitary function. The others can serve as complete window treatments.

You may combine these with curtains—a window shade behind cafe curtain or tie-backs, open shutters with fabric curtains shirred on the back, Venetian blinds with curtains covering them. If you want to block a view the shutters or vertical blinds that can be opened to let in a little daylight will function fabulously. To show off a view the shade or slender-slatted blinds will be best.

In the children's room the window is not meant to be an obstacle. The best decorating rule of thumb is to keep it simple so that the window blends in with the room rather than standing out. And keep the window safe, well locked to prevent any accidents.

ALL ABOUT WALLS

What to do with your walls? For the child's room these are definitely the most important surface in any design plan, judging by square footage alone. For the younger child the walls are the area where color can make its greatest statement. In a teenager's room it may be just these surfaces that must begin to reflect a growing maturing—these four walls that must grow up with the child.

In planning a design for the walls you will have basically four different possibilities (or any combination of these)—painting, paneling, applying fabric or wallpaper. Each of these treatments has its advantage and corresponding disadvantage. What you will want will depend once again on the budget limitations you have, the design format, and the length of time you plan to live in the location.

There's nothing like a coat of bright *paint* to give a quick pick-up to a tired room. Paint is cheap. It's colorful. It comes in a variety of finishes. (See page 69 for the things you can do with paint on the walls.)

Covering the walls with *fabric* is a more costly project but a very dramatic one. Whether you choose to shirr the fabric or hang it as you would wallpaper (see page 68) the greatest cost is the price of the fabric itself and the labor if you are not tackling this as a do-it-yourself job. Remember that in young children's rooms fabric will get its share of abuse with many dirty little hands to touch it. Unless it can be removed and washed it may be a problem.

Paneling is another costly but permanent way to cover up unsightly walls or to introduce an element of architectural interest into an otherwise dull setting. At one time a very expensive custom carpentry job, paneling is now within the reach of most families thanks to the plywood industry. These panels are made to look like more expensive varieties of wood such as mahogany, pine, and rosewood. You have just as many options with paneling as with paint or paper. You may choose to panel one or two walls rather than the entire room. If a dark wood finish is not appropriate because the room is too dark you may select one of the brightly colored panel finishes or even a sculptured effect. Paneling is easy to maintain. It can be washed and has a very long life.

Wallpaper enables you to introduce color and pattern simultaneously. Depending on what wallpaper you select it can be an extremely costly or relatively inexpensive undertaking.

You can pick out a wallpaper that is both prepasted and pretrimmed and equally simple to remove (strippable), thereby eliminating two problems—the high cost of installing and the landlord's objections to the paper itself.

With wallpaper as with other wallcoverings you have the option of covering the entire room, including the ceiling (although it is not suggested to put a pattern with a definite top and bottom on the ceiling) or to limit it to one wall and borders or any combination thereof. You can mix and match. Paint two walls and paper two. To help you make an intelligent choice at the wallpaper store, here following is a brief but comprehensive glossary of the terms you will come across browsing through the books of wallpaper patterns.

ALL-OVER PATTERN: The effect produced by a wallcovering pattern in which the units of design are evenly distributed over a surface, without undue emphasis.

BORDER: A narrow strip around an edge. A border wallpaper is used for trimming generally just under the ceiling.

COLORWAY: The combination of colors in which a design is printed. Any given design usually comes in from two to six colorings.

COMMEMORATIVE DESIGN: Designs in which a historic event or person is memorialized.

COMMERCIAL: Manufactured in quantity to serve low-priced markets.

COMPANION DESIGNS: Set of two designs created and colored to be used together in the same or adjoining areas. One is often a large and bold pattern, the other a texture or stripe.

DOCUMENTARY: A design based on a document or fabric of the nineteenth century or earlier.

EMBOSSING: A raised effect created when metal rollers impress a design into the back of a wallcovering.

ENGRAVING: Machine printing of wallcovering with etched-out rollers to get subtle and fine effects.

FLOCK: Wallcoverings imitating the surface of damask or cut velvet.

FOIL: A very thin sheet of flexible metal on a paper or fabric back.

GRASSCLOTH: Originally a hand-made product imported from Japan made by gluing grasses onto paper backing. Printed wallcoverings or dimensional ones, especially vinyl that simulate same.

MATCHING: Hanging strips of wallcovering so design is in correct relation to adjacent strip.

PREPASTED: Adhesive applied to back of wallcovering. Dipping in water before hanging activates paste.

PRETRIMMED: Wallcovering rolls from which selvage has been trimmed at factory.

REPEAT: Distance from center of one motif of a pattern to the center of the next.

ROLL OF WALLCOVERING: A bolt consisting of 36 square feet of wallcovering of which 30 square feet is estimated as usable. Bolts come in single, double, triple rolls.

SCENIC: A pictorial wall design, also called mural.

SILK SCREENING: Also called hand-screening. A printing process for wallcovering using silk tightly stretched on frames, a separate screen used for each color.

SIZE: Sealer used to prepare wall before hanging the wallcovering.

STRIP: A length of wallcovering cut to fit height of wall.

STRIPPABLE: A chemically treated stock tough enough to resist tearing, with a special formulation which permits a release of the covering from the adhesive. This makes it possible to remove an entire strip from the wall without setting.

VINYL: In the manufacturing of wallcoverings, vinyl is either a flexible film or a liquid.

VINYL COATING: Liquid vinyl applied to backing material, usually paper or fabric. After application, the product is passed through a heated oven to bond the two materials together.

VINYL LAMINATE: Vinyl laminated to either paper or a woven or non-woven mat fabric.

The vinyl flooring adds pattern and pizzazz to these boys' rooms. *Right*, designer Ruben de Saavedra outlines a blue spattered tile with red stripping. *Below*, an X marks the spot where hidden treasure is buried on a pirate's island.

A checkerboard of carpet tiles puts pattern on the floor. The orange, gold, and green tiles cushion noise as well as falls. The tiles also cover cubes for play and make a handy bulletin board around the window frame.

Cowboys and Indians, a favorite fantasy game, becomes a favorite wall cover-up in the room, *opposite*. A pair of wall hangings make an amusing impression on a bright yellow background.

Windows rate special treatment.

Top, the window wall of an apartment bedroom can be closed off completely with shutters or opened as shown with shades to pull down for privacy.

Windows that touch at right angles, *center*, get an identical twin treatment from designer Jane Victor with shades and a scalloped valance.

Cafe curtains, *bottom*, wrap around the walls for a fanciful touch.

The bedspread influences the window as well as the wall treatment, *right*. The parade figures have been cut out and appliqued on the window shade. Colors from the print repeat in a rainbow graphic at the head of the bed.

A cut-out train rides across the window shade, *left*, which is set into a frame upholstered in a print to coordinate with the rest of the room.

The walls get special treatment in the teenage girl's bedroom, *above*. A lambrequin covered with fabric frames the window wall, eliminating the need for curtains. A folding screen hides the air-conditioning unit. The wall opposite the bed is mirrored to expand the horizons of the room and is fitted with a ballet practice bar. By designer Blanche Goodman.

A sheet is the inspiration for the compact kid's room, *opposite*, designed by Shirley Regendahl. A blowup of the flower is painted right on the wall.

98

More imagination than money goes into the planning of rooms like these where the design accent is on the walls. *Opposite top*, a platform is the base for a super graphics rainbow that floats above the bed. Patterned sheets are used for shades and bed bolsters.

A campaign style bed, *opposite bottom*, gets a nautical send-off with sailboat designs cut out from self-adhesive paper.

Above, the great outdoors comes inside, complete with treehouse retreat and picket fence.

HOW TO BUY FURNITURE

Just as planning a layout is basic to the success of your room, learning the facts of life about furniture is equally essential.

From the consumer point of view, an investment in furniture even in a child's room represents a sizeable cash outlay. You will want to buy the best you can at the most reasonable price and you will want to be aware of the pitfalls and frauds.

Fact One: Generally, there are no guarantees on the sale of furniture. This means that unless you are the victim of a fraud and can prove it or unless the furniture is damaged on delivery (the company usually has insurance for this common occurrence) you will not get your money back even if the furniture falls apart. With mattresses there can be an exception.

Fact Two: The delivery of furniture is notoriously terrible. What you see on the showroom floor is a sample. Once you decide to buy ask if the item is in stock. If not, ask what the delivery date is. You may be staggered to learn that it will be months before it is available. This is because the furniture industry does not gamble with profits—they build to order and consequently get far behind with back orders. In addition, the furniture you order has to be trucked from the factory to your area.

Even with cribs this can be a problem. You may want to settle for a showroom piece rather than special ordering when time is at a premium.

Fact Three: Furniture, wood in particular, comes in all different finishes from dark and light stains to multi-colored paints. Now even Formica pieces are available in a wide range of decorator colors.

Fact Four: Furniture is styled as period design. That means a bookcase can be adapted to represent any historical period. If your room has a country feel you will probably want one of the informal periods such as the number one favorite, Early American. A more formal or fanciful room would require a French or Italian style. These you must remember are generally adaptations, not reproductions which are line for line copies of antiques.

Consider the pieces for the room:

1. *The bed:* In shopping for the bed your first priority is to buy a high quality mattress and boxspring. To buy a bed that will last through teenage years you will have to spend money. Take advantage of sale time to save. Boxsprings and mattresses regularly go on sale at major department stores. If you buy from a respected dealer and if you get a name brand there may be a

warranty or guarantee with the mattress. For a custom bed you might choose a foam mattress to be put on top of a plywood base for support.

The support for the boxspring and mattress can be anything from the floor or a simple metal frame on casters to an elaborate four poster. Headboards are often sold separately and bolt onto the metal frames.

Besides the basic bed there are also on the market a number of custom units for sale. These designs are as imaginative as can be. One company will build a chuck wagon, car, or fire engine to order as a bed. Or they will construct what they call a total environment—a sleeping unit with play area, desk, and reading area all built-in. Another design group specializes in built-up beds such as platform arrangements or loft beds on stilts.

Obviously these are very expensive compared to the cost of a basic mattress and frame. But you may find that they fill the bill for your personal needs.

2. *The chest of drawers:* The chest may be either a prefinished wood piece or an unpainted one that you will paint and repaint over the years. Look before you buy. Make sure the drawers pull in and out easily and that they are on runners that will hold them firmly. Actually examine the drawer itself to see if it is made of wood, compressed paper, plastic, or some other material. Good quality wood is obviously preferable, certainly better than paper.

Consider the size and height of the piece. A highboy (a chest-on-chest unit that goes well above the waist) is not sensible for a child because he cannot reach the top drawers. You may want a single or a double dresser style.

Make sure that the hardware (drawer pulls) is secure and will stay that way. The chest should be sturdy so that it will not pull over on the child. Watch for sharp corners on the pieces. That can mean danger for the youngster.

If you buy a chest that comes with accessory pieces that you plan to order at a later date (such as a chest that comes with a shelf unit to set on top) make sure that the style will not be discontinued. You may not be able to match the finish when you want to.

One other tip: examine the construction of the chest. Furniture that is dovetailed is superior to that put together exclusively with nails.

3. *Easy chair:* With a chair the most important thought is that the fabric be washable, even scrubbable. The chair will get a lot of abuse. A recliner is good for reading, relaxing, studying. A club chair and ottoman will also function well. Before you order the chair have your child sit in it to make sure it is comfortable for him.

4. *Desk and chair:* The simpler the better! For a desk to function well you want a good work surface and adequate drawer space and a durable finish on the work area itself. You may be attracted by a desk with all the trimmings such as pigeon holes, drawers to the floor on both sides, a decorative railing. These extras are not necessary.

The chair should be comfortable, though not too comfortable! If your child is growing you may think about a swivel chair with an adjustable height that will grow up with him.

SHOPPING SECOND-HAND

While you should never buy certain used bedroom items—a mattress, for example—there's no reason why second-hand store finds can't fit nicely into the scheme of things.

Be super cautious when you shop this way. Turn a chair upside down checking all the legs, the seat, the back. Examine a chest thoroughly just so that you know what you are getting. If you are tempted at an auction make sure you look at the piece very closely before bidding. Never bid unless you know just what you are bidding for.

Take a skeptic's position when you are being offered a genuine antique at a bargain price. You are about to be taken.

If the piece you buy needs refinishing you may do so with any number of different approaches.

But first you must put the piece in proper condition to take the new color or stain. You may have a "stripper" in your area. This is a concern that will dip the entire piece in a chemical vat to remove the layers of finish. For a delicate wood this would be disastrous but for a heavily coated piece that was inexpensive it might be worth taking the dip or you will have to invest a lot of elbow grease to get the piece in proper shape.

To prepare furniture for refinishing:

1. Remove old finish if in bad shape with a paint remover. Fill in cracks. Sand if needed.

2. If not in bad condition you can prepare the piece by washing with detergent to remove wax and dirt and then going over it with a paint thinner.

If you are antiquing the piece follow directions on the kit taking off all the hardware before you begin. To paint you will need several coats for a good finish.

Fun furniture for the child who yearns for the authentic prop. From the top, a covered wagon, racing car, and truck. These are expensive, custom-order beds.

Practical child-sized furniture, for games, parties, or reading.

The headboard is the thing, *at left*. Useful as well as decorative it is a perpetual calendar and bulletin board.

For optimum function, chests that are separate but designed to fit together, *below*, are a good investment. They may be topped off with shelves.

The modular miracle permits you to combine different units for a common cause. *Above*, furniture in the campaign style fits together to complete a room in one piece. Better yet, when needs change the pieces come apart to form different patterns.

Another version of the modular bed unit, this one, *left*, with the bed on the floor.

107

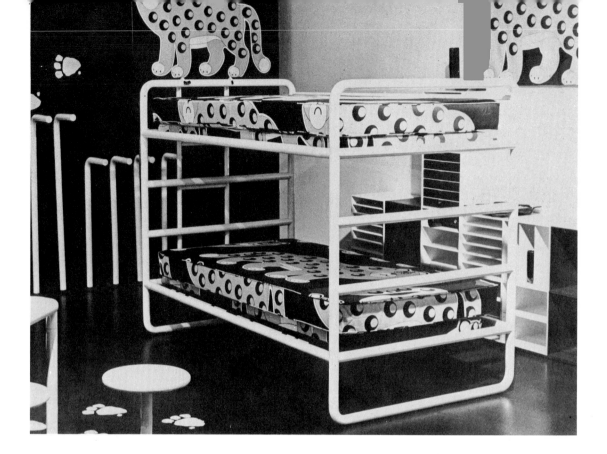

In the market for bunk beds? Be certain that there are guard rails for the upper berth and that the bed is well balanced so that it will not tip over when bedtime turns into playtime.

Desks can be found to accommodate the child. *Top*, the chair may be raised or lowered to suit the youngster's height. *Below*, the desk surface itself can be raised as the child grows.

The total environment design, *left*, is one unit designed to fit all needs. This one has sleeping quarters, study area, play space, and storage.

The bed's the thing here. *Above*, twins in a gay plaid. *Below*, a day bed style for a teenage room.

110

CHAPTER **10**

THOSE EXTRAS-
BATHROOM AND PLAYROOM

Children are little people. And people no matter how little cannot be confined. Consequently be prepared. Your children will probably love their rooms. They will sleep there. Play there. Rest there. But they will also make their presence felt in other rooms in your home.

You really wouldn't want it any other way. You can try to teach your youngsters to have respect for the home. You can try to teach them not to play in the dining room or throw balls in the living room. But you will be successful only if you do make provisions for them to play elsewhere. They will need more than anything else two special areas—a bathroom to themselves and a playroom or play area.

THE BATHROOM

What you will want to plan in your children's bath will depend on their ages. To little children a bathroom connotes splashing. Bathtime is funtime and with fun at toddler and preteen years water has a way of finding its own level. That isn't necessarily where you expect it.

In the Scandinavian countries where func-

tional living is synonymous with good design, the bathrooms are planned without the benefit of shower curtains but with a huge drain centrally located in the middle of the tiled bathroom floor.

There is another drain in the bath and shower but the additional floor drain makes it easier to cope with the floods and spill-over. You may not have the luxury of starting from scratch with your bath. Then the best advice is to make the bathroom as waterproof as possible.

Carpeting with a wall-to-wall bathroom rug is a terrible idea. It will be waterlogged and dirty most of the time. Better to leave the floor bare with a small washable throw rug near the tub. On the walls the most waterproof material is tile. This should be up the wall to at least six feet at the shower area and even better around the entire room. Tiling can be expensive but it is a permanent step and the brightly patterned Italian and Mexican tiles are lovely for a lifetime.

Next to tiling the walls, in practical order, comes paint, then vinyl wallpaper.

In the young child's bath you must observe basic safety rules. Keep all soaps, detergents, and bathroom cleansers out of the room. Make certain that medicines are not only out of reach but also locked up. And in the bath tub you will need a rubber mat to prevent slipping.

If the bath does not have a built-in hamper buy one. Encourage your child to use it. This will teach housekeeping responsibilities from the very early years. The little ones will also need foot stools so they can reach the sink and even the toilet. Paint these to match the room.

The teenager's bathroom will have different prerequisites. At this age a well lit good mirror is first and foremost. There should be space to store beauty products, cosmetics, shaving equipment.

Once you have selected a color scheme you can begin. Because the bathroom is small and hopelessly predictable it is a fun place to experiment with zany ideas. You might paint polka dots all over the walls or stencil animals or paint stripes or flowers. If it's a wallpapered room you might select a wild pattern just for shock value—though not so wild that you will hate it within weeks. To coordinate the design use accessories. First you will need a plastic waste basket—teens will use it as intended but youngsters store all water toys there. Cover the tissue box in a fabric to match the room. Make a cleanser cover out of an oatmeal container and cover that to match also in a teen's bath. In a child's bath you might get a theme from the many juvenile towels on the market. For the teenager make your own shower curtain from a gay pattern and cut out the larger print. Stitch this cut out onto your own shower towels for a custom look.

Brighten up the bath if it has a window with hanging plants.

THE PLAYROOM

Do you have a basement? Or an extra room? That's ideal if you are willing to turn it over to the children. If not even an alcove will suffice. If your child's room is small the playroom will be the area to which he will gravitate when friends are over—his social hall.

For the young child you will want a table and chairs (child size), convenient shelves for storage, perhaps a blackboard and easel. When the child approaches teen years this area will become the recreation room with furniture approximating that of the family room. The typical furnished basement fills the bill. There's plenty of floor space (for playing when young and dancing when older), comfortable sofas, chairs, small end tables, a bar for soft drinks, and a ping pong or pool table. If possible the room should be paneled with storage area behind panelled doors.

If you live in a two story home you may want to create a small play area for your youngsters on the first floor near the kitchen so that they can be watched while you work or entertain. Children like to be part of the action when they are little. In this area you might include a toy chest and a wall of pegboard to hang some play objects.

A familiar face brightens the bath, *above*. Good old Mickey Mouse in shades of red, white, and blue, turns the bath into a child's delight.

A playroom corner becomes a perpetual party area with paint, fabric, carpet, and wallpaper. Heavy duty cardboard tubing becomes columns that support a pink and white ticking tent. An old trunk is covered with wallpaper to house a menagerie of stuffed animals. Tubing stools are topped with carpet shag.

An extra upstairs room in an old house converts to a playroom with a fresh coat of paint, shag carpet, and the basics in child-sized furniture.

A tiled bath benefits from a youthful color scheme with polka dots on the wallpaper paired with stripes on the laminated window shade.

An alcove, *left*, converts to a playroom simply with the addition of child-size table and chairs, etagere to hold toys, and juvenile wallcovering.
Below, a maid's room in an old home becomes a charming playroom. Designer Larry Deutsch personalizes window shades with daughter's initials boldly emblazened in red on white.

A makeshift playroom, *left*, establishes itself at the rear door entrance. This space, adjacent to the kitchen, is ideal tot's territory—close to the cook, but not underfoot.

It's playtime at the top of the stairs, *right*. This hall in an old home gets new life with shelves lined with toys and games.

Below, attic space is reclaimed for a child's room and play area.

CHAPTER 11

EASY YOU-DO-IT PROJECTS

Brightening up your child's room can be a family project when you work together on simple yet effective do-it-yourself ideas. In this chapter a selection of original and charming, and practical, projects are presented. They vary in degree of difficulty so make sure that you read the instructions before beginning something you may not be able to finish.

PICKET FENCE

This toddler's room whimsically decorated with nursery characters calls on a white picket fence to keep things in order. To make the fence:

MATERIALS: 18¾″ by 5″ clear pine board (length is determined by measuring from floor to top of baseboard molding to one foot above the mattress).

jigsaw
scissors
pencil
brown paper
sandpaper
paint

1. Draw desired curve on brown paper and cut out.
2. Using the paper pattern, draw the top curve on each of the eighteen boards.
3. Using a jigsaw, cut board along the curve line.
4. Sand smooth and paint.
5. Fasten boards to the wall, using six boards

for the head of the bed and twelve for the side. (It is best to fasten each board in two places—2" above the base and 2" below the top of the mattress. The type of fastener depends upon your wall construction.)

POSTER BED

This young lady's room gets a lift from a frankly fake four poster bed wallpapered in a coordinated print to match the room. To make the four poster:

HEIGHT: 7'6"

Length and width of canopy and frame depend on bedding size.

For posts use 4" by 4" pine posts.

For canopy frame use ½" plywood, 6" wide.

Posts are anchored to the floor with "L" brackets on the inside of each post.

Canopy is nailed to the posts with finishing nails.

After construction wallpaper the entire unit.

SPORT'S COMPARTMENTS

This is a room which two brothers must share happily. The bed units help them live separately but equally. To construct:

1. Build or buy bookshelves to place behind the head of the standard twin beds. Paint each shelf a different color.

2. Cabinets at foot of bed are also bought or built to fit width of beds. They store sports gear.

3. The units under bed may be either the ready-made campaign style beds with drawers to store blankets or you may buy unpainted cabinet units to fit.

4. Another suggestion for the shelf units is to buy ready-made "broom closets" or cabinets with doors. They must be bolted to bed frame or they will topple.

5. Striped carpet is made from mill ends taped together. You will need heavy duty carpet knife to cut to fit.

MAKE A SIMPLE TABLE SKIRT

For a children's play table or one in the bed-room:

1. Measure the diameter of the table top. Add to this double the height of the table plus 4″ for a 2″ hem. This will give the large diameter for the skirt.

2. Spread a sheet on the floor. Make a compass with a string, attached to a pencil, and measure out a circle with this diameter. Remember the radius for the string will be half of the diameter. Then cut out the circle, hem, trim, and voila!

SEW A SLEEPING BAG

Up in the attic a secret retreat for the teen-agers is a special place for overnight parties. It's all easy to maintain with colorful sleeping bags. To sew:

1. Use two full size sheets (for standard twin bed) and a double layer of fiber-fill for extra fluffiness.

2. Baste the double layer of fiber-fill to the wrong side of one of the two sheets. (Cut the fiber-fill to size of sheet.)

3. Place second sheet (right side to right side) on first sheet, pin and baste in place.

4. Machine stitch three sides of the four layers (two sheets and two layers of fiber-fill) together.

5. Trim seams and turn sheets right side out. Fold in edges of open side and stitch closed.

6. Continue top stitching around other three sides.

7. Tack the four layers together at approximately 1½′ intervals (this will hold the layers together and give the sleeping bag extra fluff).

8. Fold in half lengthwise and stitch an 80″ zipper (Velcro tape or a tape of snaps 80″ long can be used) beginning along foot of sheets, working around the corner and up the open side.

SEW A ROOM WITH SHEETS

This frilly room was put together with sheets stitched up for the occasion. The mirror was mounted in a wood plywood frame upholstered with sheeting fabric. The fabric was stapled on.

Bed canopy and draperies:

Here the top stretchers of a four-poster canopy bed frame were used in an unconventional manner as shirred rods for a bed canopy and draperies. Rather than have the rod run through the fabric as is the custom, the designer chose to have the rod wrapped in contrasting fabric and then to have the fabric canopy stapled to the rod (stretcher).

The canopy top is a piece of sheeting cut to a size 2″ wider and double the length of the bed. Attached to this are both the draperies and the

ruffled valance. To make the ruffle valance, seam 10″ wide strip of sheeting together to form a strip which is equal to four times the length of the bed plus four times the width of the bed. The bottom edge of this entire strip should be bound with a contrasting tape. The top edge of the valance should be gathered evenly on a two-to-one basis—i.e., if your valance is 20′, you'll need 40′ of material.

Draperies to wrap around the four corners of the bed should be cut to measure 48″ in width. Their length should equal the distance from the top of the canopy to the floor (if a ruffle is added as shown here, reduce this length by the ruffle width).

These four draperies can be trimmed with ruffles as was the window swag. The top of each of the draperies should also be gathered on a two-to-one basis. Once the draperies and valance ruffle are completed, take the bed canopy top and gather the two long sides on the same two-to-one ratio used to shirr the valance and draperies. Next the canopy top, draperies, and ruffled valance can all be seamed together and laid over the bed stretchers. Or taken one at a time, first the canopy top, second the draperies, and third the ruffled valance can be stapled to the wood frame. If seamed together and laid over the bed stretchers, the draperies, valance, and canopy top will need to be carefully lined up to ascertain correct placement.

Bed dust ruffle

To fashion the bed dust ruffle, measure the distance from the head of the bed, around the foot of the bed, and up to the head of the bed again. Next measure the distance from the bottom of the mattress to the floor.

The dust ruffle shown calls for one strip of fabric which is 9″ long by two times the distance measured around the bed. The second ruffle tier should be 1″ longer than the mattress-to-floor measurement by two times the distance measured around the bed. The lower edge of each of these strips should be finished with a contrasting binding.

Once the lower edges are bound, place the shorter tier face up on top of the longer tier which should also be face up. Line up the raw edges and seam them together ¼" in from the raw edges. Next, using the two pieces of fabric as if they were one, fold 1" under. Press this in place, at the same time pressing under the raw edges along the ¼" line sewn previously. Next, sew this fold down, thus forming a tunnel through which a ½" wide piece of elastic can be drawn. Cut elastic equal in length to the distance measured around the three sides of the bed plus three feet. Run the elastic through the tunnel, join the two ends of the elastic, and slip the dust ruffle on the bed.

SEA-WORTHY ROOM

For the nautical youngster design a seascape:
1. Sails are cut from sheets in a ripply pattern.
2. Sails are supported by painted poles.
3. Waves are actually cut from carpeting to climb above bunks outlined in rope for emphasis.

NAUTICAL TREAT

Here a sailor's dream come true: Window special is curtain framed with carpet tubes painted and wrapped in nautical line.

MUD ROOM SPECIAL

To make a mud room that is colorful and a budget bonanza take a hint from this picture: For storage, use a rack of drums sprayed in primary colors inside and outside, mounted on the wall to hold boots and other outdoor gear.

SHADOW BOX UNITS FOR BED

This teenager's room shows off a collection of Indian artifacts. To make the display cabinets:

1. Display cabinets were made of ½″ plywood facing over 1″ by 10″ white pine frame, shelves, and boxes.

2. Make easy rectangular boxes with hinged tops from plywood to use for night tables with hidden storage.

3. Shadow boxes are lit with tube light and painted in different colors.

INDEX